HOW TO
DESIGN AND
PLAN A HOUSE
OR EXTENSION

GEORGE BAXTER

The right of George Baxter to be identified as author of this
Work has been asserted by him in accordance with sections
77 and 78 of the Copyright, Designs and Patents Act 1988.

PUBLISHED BY OVOLO BOOKS

Text © George Baxter 2012
This edition © Ovolo Books Ltd 2012
Printed in the UK
by Berforts Information Press

ISBN 978 1 9059 5928 0

For more information please visit
www.ovolobooks.co.uk
info@ovolobooks.co.uk

CONTENTS

CHAPTER 1

CHAPTER 2

CHAPTER 3

CHAPTER 4

CHAPTER 5

CHAPTER 1

ADVANTAGES OF GOOD DESIGN

After nearly 25 years as a Chartered Architect designing people's new homes, extensions and alterations, I've found that most people don't truly appreciate the importance of good design. However, by the time they've gone through the design process – and had the chance to see and enjoy the results – their comments often reflect deep satisfaction.

WHAT IS GOOD DESIGN?

Here are the tests I use for good home design, which apply equally to new

'The time spent discussing what we really wanted was invaluable.'

'We simply hadn't thought of what you eventually came up with.'

'We were so pleased we decided not to extend but sold up and moved to something with far greater potential.'

'We had preconceived ideas about using timber-frame construction. It was only after we had been through the design process that we decided to use a 'traditional build' method, which has proved far more appropriate for our new home and to our future requirements.'

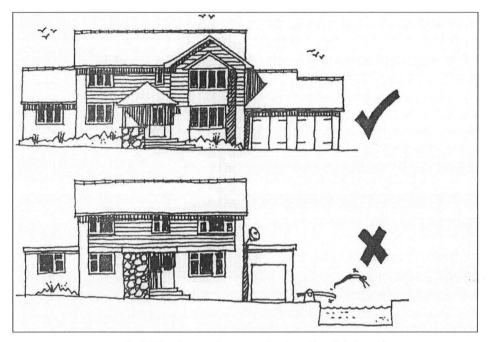

Fig 1.1 Two houses, the top one is a 'considered' design

homes, extensions or alterations.
A good design makes the most of its
location. It's vital to get rooms in the
right place – family rooms, kitchens,
living rooms are all areas where you
spend a lot of time so they should have
the best views and make the most of
the sunshine. I've seen people living on
the wrong side of a house because the
room in that location happens to be the
right size for a living room, say, despite
the traffic noise and no sunshine. New
homes are often built in the wrong
location on a potentially beautiful
site. Over-development occurs where
someone tries to build too large a house
on too small a plot.

A well-designed new home or
extension takes careful account of
the spaces around it. This prompts
consideration of prevailing wind
direction, orientation to the sunshine
and potentially pleasant places to
sit, which are sheltered and private.
Good design also considers trees
and vegetation, not only in terms of
their potential effect on foundations
(see Chapter 3), but also in terms of
overshadowing.

A good design uses the right
materials and construction detail.
There's usually a marvellous richness of

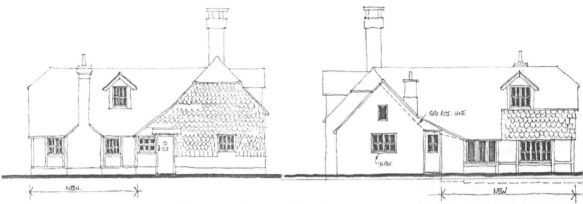

Fig 1.2 A good example of an in-keeping extension

detail and local character in most areas and these are too often missed. For me, materials and detailing are probably the most important factors in good home design and we'll return to this later (see Chapters 6 and 7).

Good design matures with age. I like to go back to look at my design projects a few years after they're completed. The right building materials will be appropriate to the particular location and correct building detail ensures the effect of rain, wind, frost and snow won't cause damage or early deterioration. If you're considering a certain material, look at a building where it's been used and has been in that location for at least five-to-ten years before you decide to use it.

Design should produce a sense of enjoyment and fun. Whenever I'm preparing a sketch design — whether it's for a new build, extension or alterations — I always try to introduce an element of delight or amusement. To do this,

consider how you live and enjoy your home. Think about including a design feature such as a bay window seat, an oriel window, a roof lantern or a panoramic window. Perhaps you could use a colour or textured material to lift the appearance of the building. It might involve changing window design or even just adding a weather vane or using interesting door handles (see Chapter 6).

Selecting the right type of construction is a component of good design. I'll go through the different methods of construction in Chapter 7. The construction stage includes the design of drainage (above and below ground), water and heating systems and the electrical system (see Chapter 9).

The design solution must meet the home owners' requirements. This implies that requirements are clearly established at the outset and provide a benchmark against which to measure the success of the final design. A good design gives

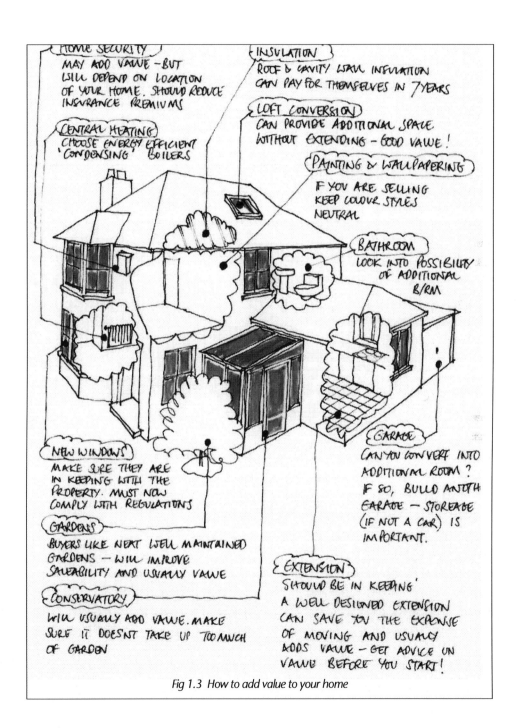

Fig 1.3 How to add value to your home

Contemporary features within a period barn conversion

priority to the most important spaces and features but takes account of all the requirements.

Finally, in assessing design, you need to be honest with yourself. The design process can be very frustrating because it can lead to conclusions you might not want to face up to. For example, having analysed a site, you could come to the conclusion that it's not suitable for what you require and you won't be happy to realise this if you've exchanged contracts. However, even in the unlikely event that this happens, on reflection, you might be grateful for the fact that you've been alerted at an early stage and didn't proceed.

GOOD DESIGN FOR EXTENSIONS

This is all the above and more. An extension either has to fit in with the building with a seamless join between existing and new or has to make a clear statement 'I'm new but I respect what has gone before'. In most cases, my measure of a successful extension is that it fits in so well with the original building that after a few years it's almost impossible to identify the extension. For example, Figure 1.3 shows an extension of a listed 16th century building where the extension picks up on the characteristics and scale of the existing property and relates to

A well-designed new one-off detatched home

the low ceilings, window size and use of materials. See if you can identify the extension.

In contrast to this approach, successful extensions can be clearly modern but respect and don't compete with the character of existing buildings. Figure 1.3 shows an example of this - a modern extension to a grade II listed property.

GOOD DESIGN FOR CONVERSIONS AND ALTERATIONS

In the case of a conversion, the proposed use has to be appropriate to the building. Over the years I've converted hundreds of buildings - water mills, threshing barns,

A new porch in keeping with the house

A well-designed modern extension

railway stations and schools - all to residential accommodation. I always ask myself whether the conversion can be done with respect to the character and heritage of the building. In most instances it's possible, with care, but not in every case.

With building alterations, it's often possible to reassess the way in which rooms are used and to improve them by introducing a design feature, such as a roof light, bay window, oriel window or feature staircase. Achieving good design can prompt major structural changes to an existing building. To the homeowner this might seem impossible, but structural

Looking out down the garden

10

Extensions and alterations in keeping with original house

alterations can transform interior space and avoid the need to extend. I remember once altering a large country house so that the kitchen remained in the same place but was opened up to the southerly aspect with access to the garden. It transformed a pokey, dark space into one of the best and most used rooms in the house. In carrying out alterations, good design involves considering everything - internal finishes, colours, lighting, fabrics and so on.

SAVING MONEY

Good design minimises maintenance costs, whether in a new build, extension or alteration. If a building design is thought through properly, in terms of its construction type and detail, it allows proper access for maintenance both inside and out. For example, gutters and down pipes are easy to get at, any material which needs maintenance is accessible, such as timber soffitts, fascias and bargeboards, and drains and pipework are within reach.

Design prompts a thought-process. Whether you're tempted to move because of inadequate space or need to alter an existing building to accommodate a changed requirement, it's always worth carefully assessing

A sensitive conversion...

what you've already got. Re-organising space or moving into a roof void can often provide answers - without all the expense of moving house. Thinking ahead is very much part of the design process and, if you allow time for proper consideration at the drawing board stage, you can save a lot of money and heartache. You're prompted to put your money where it matters, to think about your priorities and then focus your attention and budget on these.

■ Energy saving — orientation, windows, insulation?

■ Complexity of structure versus

economy of building cost?

INCREASING VALUE AND SALEABILITY

Having the right location, the right floor

area with the optimum range and size of bedrooms, reception rooms, kitchen and bathrooms, the right range of accompanying facilities and the right position and orientation within the site make a huge difference to market value and saleability. If you have any interest in the value of your home (and who doesn't?), you must bear these points in mind. The difference between getting it wrong and getting it right can be measured in hundreds of thousands of pounds. A highly idiosyncratic design or bizarre arrangement of accommodation might suit you but your architectural boldness might come back to haunt you when you sell. When designing houses, I always work with a good local estate agent (as well as the client, of course) and recommend you do the same. An agent is the best person to assess the effect on value and saleability of your choice of location and design. If you find a building plot, take advice from an agent on what would achieve best value — you never know when you'll need to sell the property.

In the case of extensions, good design balances the size of the extension with the scale of existing building and surrounding garden as it's possible to overdevelop a site and thereby lose value and adversely affect saleability. I've now extended my own house three times and on each occasion I can tell you

I was very anxious about the money I was spending in relation to the overall market value. However, the estate agents assured me it's in an excellent location — a 'sought-after' village with good rail and road links — and the site could take a bigger property. The house has gone from a small cottage to a large family house, while retaining its investment value, underpinned by its location.

With alterations, there are almost infinite installations and finishes that can add value to an existing property and also make it more saleable. Again, speak to your local agent before spending money on, for example, stripped wooden floors, a well-fitted kitchen, a sound system, a garden makeover, a conservatory, a home office or a pool enclosure. In my experience, certain alterations have an impact and add value whereas others are insignificant and can even reduce value.

The following home design factors influence market value, starting with the most significant:

■ number of bedrooms
■ size of reception rooms
■ space and fittings in the kitchen
■ number of reception rooms
■ utility space
■ external appearance

13

■ internal décor (although tastes may vary)

■ thermal efficiency

■ garden design

■ garaging

■ tennis court

■ swimming pool

MAKING MONEY WITH YOUR HOME

If you are considering building a swimming pool, try to go the whole way and have a covered, heated one. If it ever becomes unwanted, it can then be converted into a home office or granny annexe, whereas an outside pool can be a positive disadvantage.

Loft conversions normally add value but make sure they are done properly with full involvement of a qualified structural engineer. Remember that putting things right later can be almost impossible without literally pulling the roof apart.

If you're going to install an en suite bathroom in a bedroom, make sure it's a comfortable, sensible size. I've seen too many examples of squashed, badly laid out facilities, which don't add value.

Similarly, knocking through sitting and dining rooms to make one large room and replacing carpets with wooden flooring might also ultimately prove unwise.

Large rooms are ideal for entertaining but reduce flexibility while wooden floors look beautiful but magnify the sound of every footstep. I've found the best improvements only add up to a third to the value of a home so do not overspend. For example a £25,000 kitchen in a house worth £80,000 won't add more than £5,000.

Generally speaking, improvements aren't usually worthwhile if you are about to move, as they'll almost certainly not be to the taste of a potential buyer — offer a price reduction instead. Covering grubby walls with cream, magnolia or white paint is normally a good idea, however. Rewiring, fixing a roof or adding central heating can also be worthwhile. Home improvements are meant to add value but there are some which, in my opinion, do the opposite.

HERE'S MY LIST OF TOP DIY DESIGN BLUNDERS:

■ knocking a kitchen and living room into one

■ re-pointing outside bricks in white or black

■ installing an open-air swimming pool in the garden

■ sticking polystyrene tiles to the ceiling

■ adding stone cladding

■ removing period details

■ concreting over a drain cover

■ installing aluminium double glazing in a period house
■ building an extension over most of the garden
■ replacing a conventional staircase with a spiral one
■ trying to turn a small house into Blenheim Palace

WHEN YOU COME TO SELL YOUR HOME, THESE ARE SOME USEFUL DESIGN TIPS:

■ aim for light, clean colours and pastel shades
■ if you're going to spend money on just n one room, make it either the kitchen or bathroom
■ doing one room might highlight how dull others look
■ an extra room means greater value but there's no point in adding a conservatory and using it to store your bike or lawnmower — furnish it and use it as part of the living space

THINK ABOUT YOUR LIFESTYLE

One of the first things I ask people intending to build their own home is, 'How do you live and how do you want to live?' I do this to avoid trying to meet their assumed requirements or offering off-the-peg solutions, because homes should be as individual as the occupants. There are opportunities through good home design to reflect, adjust and change lifestyle.

A FEW EXAMPLES ILLUSTRATE THIS.:

■ The Jenkins family, with four children, bought a house that was clearly too small but they couldn't afford to extend. Rooms were full of storage boxes and furniture, seriously affecting all their lifestyles, resulting in chaos and arguments. By carefully examining the spaces, considering priorities and converting existing garage space into living accommodation, we reduced stress for the whole family without the need to extend the property.
■ The Jones family, with seven children, live in a lovely old farmhouse. Originally, most rooms were relatively small and dark. It was all a bit cramped and depressing inside. The family spent most of their time in the kitchen and so wanted more space in that area where the family could congregate. The solution was to build a garden room extension off the kitchen, featuring a lot of natural light and a view of the garden. The additional space has transformed their lives.
■ Mr and Mrs James are recently retired and wanted to build a home to suit their new circumstances. The thought-process in developing the design prompted them to consider in detail their new lifestyle. This resulted in a design for a low-maintenance chalet bungalow with ground floor bedroom, occasional

bedrooms for visiting grandchildren and a veranda which relates to their main interest, the garden.

Good design leads, not only to greater involvement in your home, but can also significantly enhance your lifestyle in the following ways.

LAYOUT AND SPACES CREATED

You'll think carefully about your priorities, for example, where you spend most of your time and which rooms come first in terms of space and location. You'll plan rooms for your long-term needs to avoid future problems, such as small bedrooms, which might be fine when children are young but will be inadequate when they grow up and want space to store clothes and possessions, do homework, watch television, and so on. Your bathroom will be at the right end of the house so no one will have to trek backwards and forwards to use it. Your kitchen, usually the centre of a home, will be big enough to promote good family relations. Many will incorporate a good size utility room so as not to have the noise of washing and drying machines in the kitchen or mud traipsed through to other rooms.

LIGHTING

You can locate rooms to make the most of natural light. If you're going to spend a lot of time in a room, you make sure it'll enjoy sunshine and the best of views and, perhaps, access to the garden. Where natural light is unavailable, your choice of artificial light and fittings is crucial and this is covered in more detail in Chapter 9. Lighting needs to be designed to suit the activity that will take place in the room. Well-designed lighting can introduce sparkle, interest and make a space a joy to be in.

STORAGE

A lack of storage space can cause chaos and, in extreme cases, it can even cause difficulty in achieving and maintaining simple hygiene. In order to promote a comfortable lifestyle, you'll need to consider storage requirements (see Chapter 4). You might choose to have large walk-in cupboards within bedrooms to give you adequate space for clothes, shoes and possessions. You can ensure your utility room and kitchen have storage space, not only for food, laundry and washing facilities but also for domestic cleaning products and equipment and whatever else you want. Similarly, what will you use your garage for? (Not for keeping your car in, obviously!) Will you store bikes, beach equipment, a workbench or items for the next boot sale? Don't forget the roof void. At the design stage, think about including an open, accessible roof structure. Equally, if you're designing a new home or a large extension, consider the possibility of a basement.

GARDENS

Don't forget the garden, which, if properly designed, can effectively provide a third or fourth reception room. Through the use of decking, landscape screening and imaginative planting, a space can be created which will transform how you live and think of your home.

We'll look at architectural styles in more detail in Chapters 5 and 6 but your choice of style and period of architecture can affect how you live. For example, historic buildings can impose limitations on your lifestyle, especially if it's a listed building, that is, a building of special architectural or historic interest. Think very carefully about buying a historic building, if you want lots of space, high standards of insulation, low energy consumption and minimum maintenance costs.

ACHIEVING GOOD HOME DESIGN

Bear these general principles in mind at an early stage:
■ understand what you want and how you want to live — think about your existing lifestyle and imagine changing it for the better
■ aim for ideals — write down and prioritise a 'wish list'
■ get good professional help at an early stage — there's enormous value in using a good designer to work with you.
■ Allow time to discuss your requirements properly and for thoughts to develop
■ look at many different options and plan ahead
■ establish a brief or schedule of requirements — use design tools and techniques outlined in later chapters to help you understand the possibilities
■ work with a good local estate agent — whether you're building a new home, altering an existing one or extending
■ there might be simple, cost-effective ways to improve your home — for instance adding storage systems or changing colours to alter the feel of a space
■ don't put off making changes — your home is a reflection of you, if it's unattractive, what is it saying about you?

CHAPTER 2
ANALYSING YOUR REQUIREMENTS

GETTING STARTED

Most people don't really know what they want - the size of extension, the style of new home or the layout of internal alterations. There are four vital points to consider before you start.

Designing a home often brings out tensions. If there are fundamental disagreements in the household, what chance will your home designer have in taking matters forward? For example, often one partner leaves the other to get on with the project because the other is too busy at work - until he or she learns of the estimated costs of what's emerging. Be clear about what you are trying to achieve. Share this with all those involved from an early stage. This chapter will help you through this fundamentally important process.

A home designer you employ can be on an ego trip. Many home owners think they are getting what they want but in fact they're getting what the home designer wants to design. Take time to select the right designer, see examples of his or her work and take up references.

A home owner once said to me, after we'd successfully finished an extensive alteration project on his home; 'You didn't actually ask us what we wanted, you asked us how we lived and how we wanted to live'. Consider your lifestyle as it is and whether you want to make any changes, for example, in the all-important location. Although some home owners think they want the idyllic house in the countryside, is it really right for their families? A house in such a location means they're going to spend all day in the car taking children to schools and activities after school. Might it be better for them to choose a more convenient location?

Plan ahead. Think five to ten years into the future. If you have children, what ages will they be? Never mind the kids, how old will you be? What are going to be your requirements then? Could you accommodate those requirements within the new, extended or altered home you're now considering? Figure 2.6 takes you through this process, prompting you to think ahead and helping you put together a brief or schedule of requirements. I've found that home owners who plan ahead and move to a location they wish to stay in, have a unique opportunity to develop, renovate, extend and organise a house over a long period and in the end achieve something very special.

FAMILY PLANNING

To help your thinking, here are a few issues a family with children face at various stages.

EARLY YEARS

Space is a serious issue and you need to think about storage of equipment:

nappies, push chairs, play mats, toys, trains, dolls houses, bikes, balls, boxes of bricks, outdoor play equipment and so on. Maybe you'll want a separate playroom, which can be supervised, or a convenient downstairs loo, perhaps equipped with a bath or shower.

MIDDLE YEARS

As children grow the space required increases as baby equipment gives way to a large TV or home cinema, personal computers, play stations, video storage, CD and DVD storage and mini disc players. Think also about the implications of schooling, including somewhere to do homework, and don't concentrate on where you want to live - consider where you want to educate your children. The length of school runs can make or break family happiness. Of course, it's up to you but, in my view, it shouldn't be more than 20-25 minutes in the car - even a 10 minute ride to and from a school is 3 hours 20 minutes a week in the car.

LATER YEARS

'We had the dream of family walks together but all the children want to do is to have friends over and play on the computer!' If you have children, where you live is vitally important. If you're out in the middle of some idyllic countryside setting, you could spend a lot of time

FIG 2.1 HOW TO WORK OUT ROOM SIZES

ROOM / AREA	ACCOMMODATION CHOICES	Average sq m	Other thoughts/idea	your sq m
KITCHEN Typical kitchen to include sink hob, oven, upright fridge etc.	Small Working Kitchen	6 (64)		
	Larger Working Kitchen	18 (193)		
	Average size kitchen / Informal family area (inc. 2 easy chairs + TV)	22 (236)		
	Kitchen / Dining to seat 4	15 (161)		
	Kitchen / Dining to seat 6	24+ (258)		
	Kitchen / Dining to seat 8	26+ (279)		
UTILITY Typical : work surface, drier, sink, freezer, washing machine	Utility (small)	6 (64)		
	Small utility & WC	9 (97)		
	Large utility & WC & shower	10 (151)		
LOUNGE Comfy chairs, TV, Hi-Fi, focal fire feature etc.	To seat 4 comfortably (small lounge)	12 (129)		
	To seat 8 (large lounge)	20+ (215)		
LOUNGE/DINING RM One room combining lounge & dining areas	Average size for 4	16 (172)		
	Lounge/dining for 8+	30 (323)		
SEPARATE DINING dining table, chairs, sideboard	dining area for 4	16 (172)		
	Dining area for 8+	30 (323)		
HALL	Small hall, access to other rooms	6 (64)		
	larger hall with feature such as staircase, full height space	12+ (129)		
	Dining hall to seat 4	14+ (151)		
	Dining hall to seat 8+	20+ (215)		
STUDY	Small study, I.e. Computer + desk	6.5 (70)		
	Larger study, computer + desk + conference area	12+ (129)		
WC	Small & basic: hand basin+ WC	3+ (32)		
	Large : coat hanging area, hand basin, WC etc	6+ (64)		

ROOM / AREA	ACCOMMODATION CHOICES	Average sq m	Other thoughts/idea	your sq m
MASTER BEDROOM	Smaller more compact double bedroom	15 (161)		
	Large double bed, clothes storage / cupboards x 2 dressing areas + easy chair etc.	25+ (269)		
ENSUITE DRESSING	Separate dressing room	6 (64)		
ENSUITE BATHROOM	Basin, WC, bath, shower	8 (86)		
FAMILY BATHROOM	to include bath, WC, bidet, wash hand basin + space	10 (108)		
CHILDRENS' SINGLE	Nursery: small bed, small desk, fitted cupboard	6 (64)		
	Larger, space for double bed, desk, cupboards	10 (108)		
GUEST BEDROOM	Double bed, dressing table, fitted cupboards x 2	14 (151)		
GAMES ROOM	Table tennis table,	26+ (279)		
	Pool table	23+ (247)		
	Full size snooker table	32+ (344)		
GARAGES	Single garage	16+ (172)		
	Double garage	40+ (430)		
TOTAL AREA (FOR NEW BUILD OR EXTENSIONS)				

Use the chart on this and the page opposite to estimate your approximate room sizes

to-ing and fro-ing collecting and delivering your children and their friends. This becomes less of an issue as children get older and can, at last, drive but, maybe by this time, they're considering moving away anyhow. Think about bedrooms with en suite facilities, taking pressure off the bathroom, and making them big enough and include a shower. Remember, the older children get, the more time they spend in the bathroom. If you've had a playroom for your young children, perhaps it could become a teenage den where they can do their own thing without parents in the way.

The conclusion I've come to is that space and how you use it is vital, through the whole experience of bringing up children. Get things right at the start and you'll find your home can expand, contract and adapt to the changing needs of your family.

Figures 2.2 & 2.3 show you how to assess your requirements and put together a brief, prompting you to consider lifestyle, future needs, initial costs and location. Work your way through this to get a better understanding of what you actually require.

COLLECTING INFORMATION

VISITING FRIENDS AND SHOW HOUSES
Make notes of design features, colours and finishes when you visit friends' houses or show houses on new estates. Ask friends how they get on with a particular layout. Compare their requirements with your own and consider whether the design solutions you see provide answers for you. Most people are only too happy to talk about how they've arrived at the arrangement of accommodation or design for their home. Learn from them and their experiences but remember comments and thoughts are easily forgotten, so it's important to write them down at the time. I suggest starting a scrapbook in which photographs, ideas, articles and snippets of information can be placed.

MEASURE THE FURNITURE
Measure the furniture you want to re-locate Measure the plan, footprint and height of furniture and fittings you want to accommodate and think about space around it needed for and access and circulation. There are simple design tools which can help you understand space requirements (see chapter 4).

MAGAZINES
Google the latest home design magazines. These publications are continually changing with new issues or re-issues in different formats. It's a good idea to take two or three magazines on

a regular basis. Most feature new and converted homes and many also show renovations, alterations and extensions. They provide much food for thought, ideas, inspiration, information on costs and useful contacts.

EXHIBITIONS AND SEMINARS

Visiting exhibitions is essential if you're contemplating a major new design project. Most major manufacturers of building materials and design products, and firms who offer design-related services are now represented at these exhibitions and anxious to discuss their various products and services with you the potential customer. Exhibitions are advertised in national newspapers, home design magazines and local media. There's also a list of dates and venues for future events online.

TV PROGRAMMES

These are enormously popular and provide not only good entertainment but also design ideas, tips and information, which can be kept on a video (often available through the networks). Make notes of websites mentioned.

BOOKS

There are hundreds to choose from – everything from coffee table books with stunning glossy photos, through books

of home plans to very down-to-earth practical books and all have their role and value. Find what suits you by browsing in bookshops, libraries or on-line book retailers. The Building Centre in London has a comprehensive bookshop, which does mail order and on-line shopping, and permanent building exhibitions.

YOUR HOME DESIGNER

If you intend to work with a home designer, such as an architect, architectural technician or building surveyor, make sure his or her work is compatible with the style of building you want - before you employ them. A good home designer should establish this with you anyway, including showing you examples of previous projects.

SHOPS AND BUILDERS MERCHANTS

Superstores (such as B&Q and Homebase and department stores are all invaluable sources of home design suggestions, possibilities and products. (The website has names and links.)

INTERNET

If you've got access to the internet, it's probably the most useful source of information. Most manufacturers, retailers, publishers and providers of services have websites with varying amounts of useful material and ideas. My

FIG 2.2 IDEAS CHART : SELECT WHAT YOU WANT		*Select by ticking*
1	KITCHEN	
	AGA / RANGE COOKER	
	BREAKFAST BAR	
	VIEWS OF GARDEN / OR FRONT DRIVE OR BOTH	
	WORKTOP BUILT IN SCALES	
	INDUCTION HOB	
	CONSERVATORY / KITCHEN / BREAKFAST ROOM	
	CENTRAL ISLAND FEATURE	
	AMERICAN STYLE FRIDGE FREEZER	
	FARMHOUSE STYLE KITCHEN (TABLE AT CENTRE OF KITCHEN)	
	SINK PRE-FORMED IN WORKTOP	
	WASTE DISPOSAL UNIT	
	HIDEAWAY KITCHEN (WITHIN CUPBOARDS)	
	CENTRAL HUB KITCHEN (IN TERMS OF OVERALL DESIGN LAYOUT)	
2	HALLS	
	FEATURE STAIRCASE : BI-FOCATED STAIR, SPIRAL, SEMI-CIRCULAR, STRINGLES STAIR	
	DESIGN DETAIL IN BALUSTRADE BULLNOSE STEP, VOLUTE	
	GALLERIED LANDING	
	STONE FLOOR FINISH	
	DINING / HALL SPACE COMBINED NEAR KITCHEN	
	FEATURE WINDOW	
	CIRCULAR HALLWAY	
	THE DINING HALL (HALL USED AS DINING ROOM)	
3	ENTRY PORCH	
	SPACE TO ACCOMMODATE? NO PEOPLE. DECIDE HOW MANY PEOPLE IT MUST SHELTER	
	STONE FLOOR	
	BUILT-IN SEATS	
4	LOUNGES	
	BAY WINDOW	
	WINDOW SEAT WITHIN DEEP WINDOW REVEALS (THICK WALLS ONLY)	
	ISLAND FIREPLACE (DOUBLE ASPECT)	
	2 AMP LIGHTING CIRCUITS (ALLOWS TABLE LAMPS TO BE SWITCHED)	
	HOME CINEMA	
	BUILT-IN HI FI	
	SLIDING / FOLDING DOORS	
	INGLENOOK FIREPLACE	
	BLINDS ENCLOSED IN GLAZING UNITS	
	POWER POINTS IN THE FLOOR	
	CHIMNEY / FIREPLACE AS ROOM DIVIDER (DOUBLE SIDED FIREPLACE)	
	CHANGES OF LEVEL OR SPLIT LEVELS, I.E. LOUNGE / DINING ROOM	
	HALL / LOUNGE, SUNKEN SEATING	
	SUNKEN BAR	
5	BEDROOMS	
	WALK-IN WARDROBES WALK 'ONTO' BALUSTRADE ACROSS FULL HEIGHT DOORS	
	BALCONY WALK 'ONTO' BALUSTRADE ACROSS FULL HEIGHT DOORS	
	ENSUITE DRESSING ROOM	
	ENSUITE BATHROOM	
	THE SLEEPING PLATFORM (AT MEZZANINE LEVEL)	
	SPIRAL STAIRCASE TO MEZZANINE LEVEL	
	THE SLEEPING GALLERY	
	BEDROOM FIREPLACE	
6	CHILDRENS' BEDROOMS	
	FEATURE BED / BUNK BED; CARTOON CHARACTER / CAR / PLANE / TRAIN / PULL DOWN BED	
	STUDY FACILITIES	

	ENSUITE FACILITIES DECIDE ON SHOWER OR BATH OR BOTH	
	STORAGE & CUPBOARD SPACE	
7	BATHROOMS	
	2 WASH HAND BASINS VANITY UNITS 'FLUSH WITH FLOOR' SHOWER	
	SHOWER FOR 2 BODY JETS	
	CURVED BATHROOM LAYOUT IN RESPECT OF APPLIANCES BUILT INTO DUCTS	
	SUNKEN / OR RAISED BATH	
	SHARED ENSUITE (BETWEEN 2 DIFFERENT BEDROOMS)	
	PAINTED VERTICAL BOARDED WALLS AS OPPOSED TO TILING	
8	ROOMS IN THE ROOF	
	ATTIC TRUSS / CUT ROOF	
	STUDY SPACE	
	ROOF WINDOWS	
	ROOF DORMER STYLE WINDOWS	
9	LANDINGS	
	USE OF SUN PIPES	
	GALLERIED LANDING	
	LINEN CUPBOARD STORAGE	
	EXTRA WIDTH LANDING TO PROVIDE ROOM FOR DESK / FURNITURE	
10	UTILITY ROOM	
	DRYER / WASHING MACHINE	
	CLOTHES HORSE	
	FITTED CUPBOARDS	
	COAT HANGING / BOOT STORAGE	
	DOG WASHING / HOSING DOWN SHOWER (FLUSH WITH FLOOR LEVEL)	
11	HEATING / CLIMATE CONTROL	
	UNDERFLOOR HEATING / TRENCH HEATING SYSTEMS	
	UNDERFLOOR HEATING IN A BATHROOM	
	PROGRAMMABLE TAPS	
	PRESSURISED DOMESTIC HOT WATER	
	WEATHER COMPENSATION / OPTIMISATION	
	AIR CONDITIONING / COMFORT COOLING	
	CONDENSING BOILER	
	IN-LINE WATER FILTER	
	IN-LINE WATER SOFTENER	
	FLAT INVISIBLE / FEATURE RADIATORS	
	ZONE CONTROLS	
	THERMOSTATIC RADIATOR VALVES	
	INSTANT (CIRCULATING) HOT WATER	
12	I.T.	
	DECT	
	PHONES	
	HOME NETWORK FACILITIES	
	TV / SATELLITE SIGNAL DISTRIBUTION	
	HOME AUTOMATION	
	BUILT-IN PLASMA SCREEN	
	CCTV AUTOLOCK ENTRY PHONE	
13	SOLAR / ENERGY CONSERVATION	
	RAINWATER HARVESTING	

	PHOTOVOLTAIC ROOFS	
	SOLAR THERMAL HOT WATER HEATING	
	LOW 'E' GLAZING	
14	SECURITY	
	ALARM SYSTEMS	
	HOME SECURITY SYSTEMS	
15	OUTSIDE	
	OUTDOOR HOT TUB	
	OUTSIDE WATER TAP	
	AUTO IRRIGATION SYSTEMS	
	ELECTRIC GATES	
	SWIMMING POOLS	
	DECKS	
	PATIOS	
16	MISCELLANEOUS ITEMS	
	UNDERFLOOR SAFE	
	BASEMENTS	
	CENTRAL VACUUM SYSTEM	
	STAINED GLASS	
	GYM / GAMES ROOM	
	FIRST FLOOR ROOF TOP CONSERVATORY	
	EXPOSED BEAMED CEILINGS	
	DEEP WINDOW REVEALS / SPLAYED WINDOW REVEALS	
	SHUTTERS IN TIMBER	
	BORROWED LIGHTS (ABOVE DOORS)	
	CLEAR STOREY LIGHTING	
	SELF COLOURED PLASTER, I.E. POLISHED PLASTER IN TERRACOTTA OR GREYS	
	CONCEALED OR POCKET DOORS BUILT INTO WALLS	
	THE MUSIC / HOME ENTERTAINMENT ROOM	
	STRUCTURAL GLASS BLOCKS GIVING PRIVACY & RETAINING LIGHT	
	POST & BEAM CONSTRUCTION : POLE FRAME TRADITIONAL / CONTEMPORARY	
	OAK ENGINEERING	
	GLUE LAM	
	STEEL	
	CIRCULAR WING OR TOWER HOUSING TO CONTAIN A SPIRAL STAIR	
	BANKS OF ROOF LIGHTS	
	INTERNAL WINDOWS	
	FEATURE RADIATORS	
	CONCEPT OF UPSIDE DOWN LIVING, I.E. LOUNGE ON A FIRST FLOOR	
	THE VERANDAH	
	THE ROOF GARDEN	

	BALCONIES	
	ARCHED OPENINGS	
	ELECTRO OPAQUE GLASS (SAINT GOBAIN)	
	PANELLING - VERTICAL TIMBER	
	LA FARGE PURPOSE BUILT MOULDED PANELLING	
	UNDERFLOOR HEATING - WARM TILE SYSTEMS - KITCHEN / BATHROOMS	

Fig 2.3 HOW TO RECORD INFORMATION AND DEVELOP A BRIEF (OR SCHEDULE OF REQUIREMENTS) FOR YOUR NEW HOME, EXTENSION OR ALTERATION

WHAT YOU DO

STEP ONE
Recording information: record information in any way that you feel happy with. For example:
a) Use scrapbooks to keep photographs, cut outs from magazines.
b) On a computer including scanned images, photographs etc.
c) In a ring binder file which makes it easy to insert and take out clippings, photographs, cuttings etc.
It really doesn't matter how you record information as long as it is accessible and not forgotten. Digital cameras make life easy in that one can record photographs of particular places you've been and then append them to a list of ideas / files.

STEP TWO
Recording your actual requirements. Go to Illustration 2.1: your approximate requirements for room sizes for a new home, alteration or an extension). Go through the various rooms / areas listed and select the room or area required. (For example, if you require a kitchen / dining room to seat 4, insert in the right hand column the approximate area and any design features / ideas.

Whilst considering a particular room, it is useful to record other design ideas. See fig 2.2: The 'Select an idea' chart prompts you to think of design ideas or features and add them to Illustration 2.1. (Again, for example, in a kitchen you might wish to add an Aga, a quarry tile, or underfloor heating).

Work through the requirements. You could also add references to your scrapbook and prompt you to remember a particular design feature or idea you have seen and noted.

STEP THREE
Consider future requirements. I generally recommend that people think ahead at least 5–10 years. Here are some of the key factors: Having children! (a need for increasing space, storage, games rooms, family rooms, second reception rooms). Retirement. Need to consider access and mobility. (Bedrooms on a ground floor, shower rooms). Business. The possibility of running your own business or providing a home office for your company. Annexe accommodation. Providing accommodation for an elderly parent or a teenager / young adult.

STEP FOUR
Consider location, location, location. Ask yourself some questions: does this location fit your requirements in terms of access to work, access to shops, access to facilities which will be needed for your children both in the short term and later on.

STEP FIVE Consider cost. Referring back to fig 2.1 assess very approximate costs using a rate per square metre (or per square foot) for new build or extensions. Building alterations are much more difficult to assess. Chapter Eight refers to design and building cost in more detail and takes you through a step-by-step sequence.   At this stage you are considering very rough ideas of costs to help you write a realistic brief.

STEP SIX Develop your 'Brief'.

Design ideas: contemporary staircase (above), curved door (top right) and Juliet balcony (right)

own site, www.homedesign-online.co.uk, promotes good design and helps you to come to the right solutions, including design solutions to typical home owners' problems, a directory and design tools.

INSPIRATIONAL IDEAS

By the time you've worked through this chapter, you should've firmed up your requirements, know how to record information and be aware of where ideas can be found. You've also got simple step-by-step procedures to draw up a brief or schedule of requirements and do be methodical in working this up. Remember, while you do need to crystallise ideas, it's important to retain flexibility. Don't dismiss your ideals - if you don't strive for them there's a danger of having none of them in your design. At

the same time, be conscious, even at the early design stage, of approximate order of cost. But, whatever else you do, the over riding message must be that a proper analysis of your requirements is essential to the process.

Design ideas: contemporary kitchen island

Design ideas: open plan living with full-height glazing

CHAPTER 3

ANALYSING YOUR SITE

Knowing what you want is the starting point but equally important is understanding and appreciating what you've got. If you're building a new home, your site might be land, which has never been built on, or a house to be demolished and replaced, maybe because it's either poor quality or too expensive to alter. When you're considering extending, your analysis will be of the building, its site and surroundings. If you're buying an existing house, you might want to assess its structure and layout for alteration and improvement potential. Where you're purchasing a property

with a view to carrying out your project, it's necessary to make an initial quick assessment in order to be able to make an offer. If your offer is accepted, it's desirable to make a more detailed and careful analysis before exchanging contracts. Alternatively, if you're looking at your existing home or land and wondering about its potential, the initial assessment should tell you whether there's scope to achieve what you want.

INITIAL ASSESSMENT

The following steps are what I usually do when making an initial assessment and are equally applicable to a plot for a new home and to an existing house for extension or alteration.

SPEAK TO NEIGHBOURS

Find time to meet and talk to your prospective neighbours about the property and area. They might have knowledge of unusual environmental conditions such as flooding, noise or traffic levels. You can learn a lot from a short conversation with someone who wants to be helpful. While you're chatting, you might also want to work out whether you'll be able to get on with these people as your neighbours.

CARRY OUT A PRE-PLANNING ENQUIRY

This involves talking to the council and researching any planning history and local plan policy for the area, especially future development proposals. In practical terms, there might well not be time to make an offer to buy a property subject to first getting planning permission. However, this doesn't stop you seeking some comfort from the council. I've found the best way of doing this is to arrange an appointment to meet the relevant planning officer for the area - don't rely on the officer being able to come out to site as they usually claim to be too busy. Have your

pertinent questions ready to ask (such as, would you allow an extension? how big an extension would you allow? what size of new dwelling would be accepted?). Make notes of what's discussed then afterwards write to the council with your understanding of the issues and ask the officer to write back to confirming this.

MAKE ENQUIRIES WITH SERVICE PROVIDERS

If you are building a new home on a virgin site, establish whether mains drainage is available by contacting the local authority's building control department or the drainage undertaker. Check also the availability of electricity, gas, water and telephone connections and costs. In a similar vein, if you're in a low-lying area contact the Environment Agency to discover whether the site is liable to flooding.

OBTAIN A PLAN

When I'm working out the space available on a site I always get an Ordnance Survey Superplan map (google OS maps). This is an individually printed site-centred plan, normally up to date, showing the outline of the site, any existing buildings and adjacent properties. It'll give you a useful perspective of your property or proposed acquisition and can be used at a later stage for making a planning application.

WALK THE SITE

Write down your first impressions, which might be very basic comments but they're important. Use the check lists (Figures 3.1 and 3.2) to help record important features. Listen for noise from sources such as aircraft, traffic or businesses. Note the prevailing wind direction and see if there are potential sources of smells upwind like farms or factories.

Take plenty of time to get a feel for the path of the sun, any noise and potential overlooking, remembering that any deciduous vegetation will loose its screening value during the winter months. Take a compass to establish where the sun rises and sets (remembering the difference in altitude during winter and summer months). Misunderstanding orientation can lead to grave design and layout errors.

The sort of initial assessment described can often be carried out within two or three days and by the end of that time you'll have a much better idea of the site you're actually buying. The time you spend on site is of the most value as it's your feel for the environment that's most important.

DETAILED ASSESSMENT

The second stage is a more detailed analysis and often involves repeating some of the activities you carried out making your initial assessment. However, it's critical at this stage to be more thorough and it might well be appropriate to employ professional help, as described later in this chapter. Figure 3.1 contains my site assessment check list for a new home. Go through this to end up with a list of design advantages and disadvantages to arrive at an overall conclusion. Figure 3.3 provides a useful check list for you to go through to help in making a decision on building an extension to an existing home.

Remember that, when looking at any site, always start with your ideal and check whether the site would provide what's required to achieve it. Many of the people I've worked with have found that what at first appeared to be an ideal site just doesn't work in terms of travelling distances and time. This comes back to location, location, location and being realistic about your needs and requirements.

We've mentioned professional help and, although there's a lot you can do yourself, there's a great deal at stake so paying for assistance can be very worthwhile and often need not cost that much. At the pre-purchase stage,

FIG 3.1 SITE ASSESSMENT FOR YOUR NEW HOME: CHECK LIST		
CHECK LIST	*POINTS TO CONSIDER*	*DESIGN OPPORTUNITY OR DISADVANTAGE*
Check if there is an accurate site survey	*See if this includes accurate levels and / or information about services. Does it accurately record boundaries, trees, landscape features.*	*A good accurate survey will enable you to consider designs at an early stage.*
Landscape features	*Trees, contours, any previous works on the site (such as underground cellars, wells are all important especially if you are building in an area where there has been previous activity. I include as landscape features any archaeological issues.*	*Are there any opportunities to incorporate a change in level in the home design.*
Overlooking	*If I build in this location will someone be able to look in and affect my privacy. Equally, if I can construct something will it overlook someone else's garden.*	*Design restriction.*
Views	*Can I make the most of these in developing my design. Where am I going to spend most of my time in my home? Where am I going to make the most of the best views.*	*Design opportunity*
Where is the sun path?	*How does the sun move around the site from the beginning to the end of the day and at different times of the year.*	*Carefully positioning patios and rooms*
Prevailing wind	*Where is going to be a place to sit outside sheltered from the wind.*	*To create a sheltered external environment perhaps using planting etc.*
Soil conditions	*Having a trial hole and getting the soil conditions analysed if you are planning to build an extension or a new home*	*Soil conditions can affect foundation costs*
Restrictive covenants	*Are there any legal restrictions on what you can do on the site*	*These will need checking out at an early stage with your solicitor or the Deeds of the property or site you are buying*
Environmental factors	*Is the site liable to flooding?*	*Severe design restriction!*
Noise, pollution, contaminated land	*Consider noise from roads or aircraft or indeed other sources such as local business industry*	*Design restriction.*
Planning	*Consider the planning history of the site and current planning policy*	*Usually a design restriction.*

NOW LIST ALL YOUR DESIGN OPPORTUNITIES AND DESIGN RESTRICTIONS IN A + AND - COLUMN TO SEE WHICH COLUMN OUTWEIGHTS THE OTHER

Good landscaping is important

whether as an initial assessment or a detailed analysis, a site appraisal, based on your carefully considered requirements, can be invaluable. It could be carried out by an architect, building surveyor, planning consultant or other design or building consultant. Whoever you employ, it's essential to brief the professional on exactly what you want to know. Key questions could relate to whether you're likely to get planning permission, whether there's enough space on site to create what you want or what the likely approximate cost would be.

Once you've decided to proceed to buy a property, what you need to do next obviously depends on whether you're building a new home or extending or altering an existing one. Firstly, let's look at building a new home. You, or your professional team, are going to need a land survey and I recommend you have this done professionally by a firm which specialises in this field. Commission a firm which uses computerised digital

Different levels create a challenge but also can provide interest and variety

equipment. This enables the surveyors to plot levels over the whole site in a quick and efficient manner and to produce an extremely accurate drawing, recording boundaries, adjacent properties, landscape features, trees, tree canopies and so on. For an acre-sized plot this could be quite expensive but you'd never do it accurately on your own. The information recorded is invaluable to any development and, in my view, no design should start without one. Supplement the survey with photographs and record where they were taken from.

In the case of altering or extending an existing home you'll always need a proper building survey. This is often done by one of your professional team, such as an architect or building surveyor. These surveys involve full accurate measurement of every room in the house and the whole building in terms of each level, vertical sections through the structure and elevations (side views of the building). All this information would be required later if formal applications

FIG 3.2 SITES FOR EXTENSIONS: POINTS TO CONSIDER

Consider all those items mentioned in figure 3.1 for a site for a new home but include also the following points:

CHECK LIST	POINTS TO CONSIDER	DESIGN OPPORTUNITY OR DISADVANTAGE
Existing structure	Where are load-bearing walls, how is weight transferred down through the building?	Remember anything is possible although certain changes will involve more work than others so an understanding of the building structure is vital. See Chapters 8 & 12
Existing drainage	Where is existing foul drainage in relation to perhaps a new bathroom or waste requirement.	Design restriction - an understanding of these restrictions is important at an early stage - see Chapter Twelve
Is the existing house listed?		DO - save VAT?
Existing fabric	General condition	DR -expensive to alter
Existing services	Drain survey; electrical test	
Effect of overlooking on a neighbour	Will an extension overlook your neighbour? Good test : would you like it?	Dr - meet your neighbours before you buy
Effect of being overlooked		DR

have to be made to the council for planning permission or building regulations approval. It's also an essential tool to any designer in considering your requirements. Building surveys can be quite expensive as they're time consuming. I always reckon that if I spend a day carrying out a measured survey, it'll take me two days to put it onto a computer plot.

If you're building a new home or a substantial extension you must get some trial holes dug on the site. A structural engineer can usually organise this with the help of a local builder. The idea of a trial hole is to check the soil conditions over the proposed new building area or where you're proposing to extend an existing property. In the latter case, a trial hole is used to examine the depth of existing foundations to ascertain whether they need underpinning in relation to a new build. Soil is usually taken from trial holes and sent for laboratory analysis. From this analysis your structural engineer will be able to tell you what type of foundations would be appropriate. This can have a big effect on cost and feasibility, as explained later in Chapter 10.

CHAPTER 4

HOW TO DESIGN

This chapter shows you how to carry out your ideas and turn them into simple design drawings. To do this you'll need:

■ two tape measures: 5 and 30 metres long to measure an average sized room and to measure a site

■ tracing paper: A3 size (60 x 42cm, roughly 2ft x 16.5in) or you can use kitchen greaseproof paper. On the tracing paper draw a grid (a series of parallel equidistant lines running and across and up and down the page) covering the whole sheet of paper. The grid represents the metric scale at which

you'll be working. For a scale of 1:50, the lines need to be 1cm (0.5in) apart and for 1:100 the lines need to be 2cm (1in) apart. Finally, get a sharp pencil, rubber, pair of scissors and some thin card. In this chapter we aim to understand basic design terminology, such as scales, plan, sections, elevations (see below)

STEP ONE

I always start the design process for an extension, alteration or new build with sketch 'doodles' or simple bubble diagrams to put on paper the various constraints and ideas that I've collected in my research on both requirements and the site (see Chapters 2 and 3). Don't worry if this becomes a messy collection of lines, arrows, bubbles or whatever else you feel happy drawing. Figure 4.1 is an example of a very simple design 'doodle' I did at an early stage in the design of a new home which was subsequently developed into a simple plan. Keep your early sketches as they are valuable and will record the direction in which the design develops.

STEP TWO

Chapter 3 mentions getting a survey

carried out professionally but you could do it yourself if you take great care. First a few technical terms.

A SCALE

Looks like a ruler but allows you to plot and draw a building in exact proportions to its actual size. You can then measure off the drawing and equate this to actual dimensions. All drawings are now metric and the scales used are usually 1:100, 1:200 and 1:50. With 1:100, 1cm (0.5in) on the drawing is equivalent to 1 metre (around 3ft 3in) of the building. 1:200 is

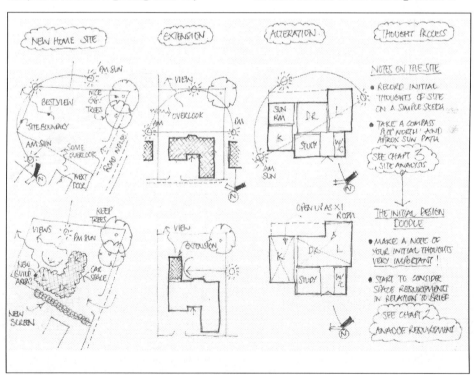

Fig 4.1 Record your first impressions

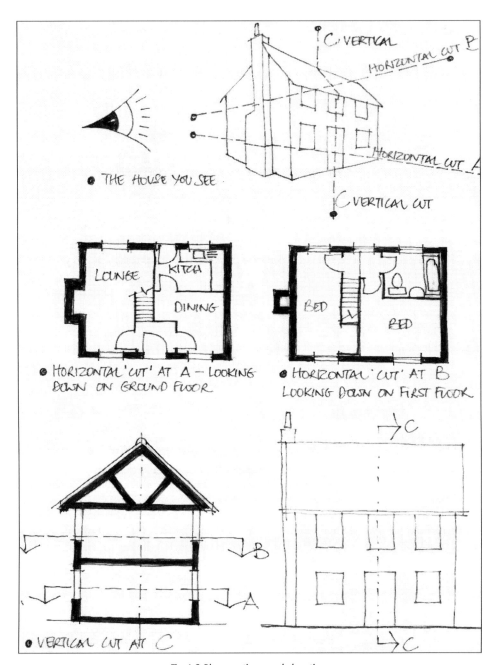

Fig 4.2 Plans, sections and elevations

a smaller scale (half the size of 1:100), where 1cm (0.5in) represents 2 metres (around 6ft 6in) and is useful for looking at your home in relation to its site. A larger scale, say, 1:50 (double the size of a drawing at 1:100), is useful when working with plans and room layouts, as 2cm (0.75in) is equivalent to 1 metre. I sometimes use a scale of 1:20 to represent building construction detail. Scales are usually shown in the bottom right-hand corner of drawings and it's a good idea to write on a plan the scale you've used.

A PLAN

This is a bird's-eye-view of the layout of any floor of a home. It's like taking a horizontal cut through the building at each floor level, usually a metre (around 3ft) above the floor. At this height it shows windows, doors, openings, walls, furniture and fittings. Walls are usually shown in heavy lines as they have been 'cut through', windows and fittings with thinner lines and doors are often shown as a quarter circle indicating the door swing (the path of the door as it opens and shuts).

A SECTION

This is similar to a plan but is a vertical cut-through view of a building. As with plans, walls, ceilings and floors are usually shown in heavy lines. Sections provide an internal view of your home and, as explained later in this chapter, can show your home in relation to its site, providing valuable information for the design process.

ELEVATIONS

These are drawings of each side or external face of a building and are normally labelled according to their orientation, for instance a south elevation shows the side of a home that faces

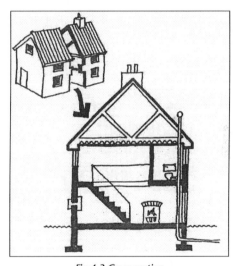

Fig 4.3 Cross section

south. Plans, sections and elevations should always be drawn to a scale and should be accurate.

HOW TO SURVEY

Figure 4:3 shows how this process works for an extension or new build. You'll need

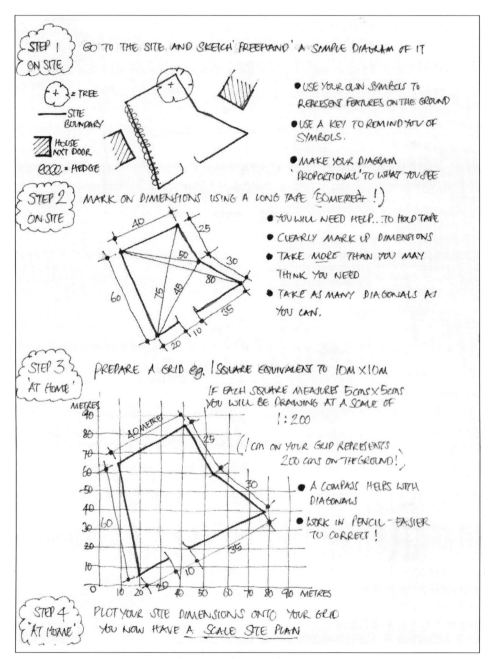

Fig 4.4 Carrying out a site survey

a long (30m) tape measure and I suggest you use the 1:200 grid, assuming an average plot size. The bigger the plot, the larger the sheet of paper needs to be. Physically measure around the perimeter of the house, recording the dimensions on paper. Then measure to fixed points on the house to boundary perimeters and also plot features such as trees and changes in level. Draw a diagram of the site and any existing building and plot dimensions clearly onto your 1:200 grid. Remember to take lots of diagonal dimensions in order to plot boundaries, because these are not normally parallel. Figure 4.3 also shows how you can plot approximate ground levels relative to your new home or extension.

If you're altering the inside of a house, you'll have to carry out a survey of the existing building, which can be done in a similar way to that described above (see Figure 4:4). Measure around the perimeter of a room plotting any changes in wall directions or fixture or fittings, windows doors etc. and then draw a plan onto your 1:50 grid. Remember to take diagonal dimensions as a check.

An extension involves a bit of both of the above scenarios. You'll need to measure up the existing building, outside and inside in the areas of the house where you're likely to extend and then plot the space outside the building where you expect the extension to be located. With an extension you can probably still use the 1:50 grid, provided you only plot the relevant part of the house and appropriate part of the site.

There's lots of sophisticated equipment and professional help available for undertaking measured surveys. I suggest you employ a specialist to carry out an accurate site survey later, if appropriate. The whole purpose of this book, and what I've described above, is to get you involved in, and to encourage a better understanding of, the design process. These DIY grid surveys enable you to do this. You will find there are relatively inexpensive laser measuring devices on the market (Google!)

STEP THREE

In order to design your new home, extension or alteration, you need to appreciate the space required for moving through your home. Allow for doorways and doors to open, corridors, space needed to move around appliances, space required for furniture and sanitary ware fittings. Remember to include cupboards and wardrobes and their doors. You must also consider storage (often forgotten) as you need space for clothing, linen and general household clutter (usually the whole of the roof void) and for various appliances used in the home and garden

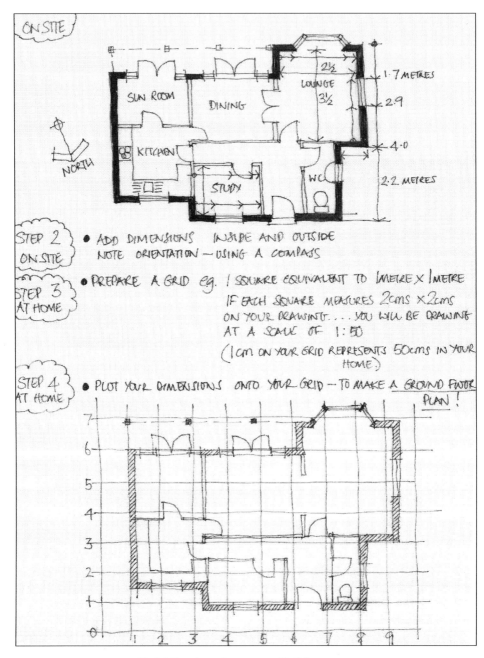

ON SITE

SUN ROOM

DINING

LOUNGE
2½
3½

1.7 METRES

2.9

4.0

2.2 METRES

KITCHEN

NORTH

STUDY

WC

STEP 2
ON SITE
• ADD DIMENSIONS INSIDE AND OUTSIDE
  NOTE ORIENTATION — USING A COMPASS

STEP 3
AT HOME
• PREPARE A GRID eg. 1 SQUARE EQUIVALENT TO 1 METRE X 1 METRE
  IF EACH SQUARE MEASURES 2cms X 2cms
  ON YOUR DRAWING ... YOU WILL BE DRAWING
  AT A SCALE OF 1:50
  (1 cm ON YOUR GRID REPRESENTS 50cms IN YOUR
                                        HOME.)

STEP 4
AT HOME
• PLOT YOUR DIMENSIONS ONTO YOUR GRID — TO MAKE A GROUND FLOOR
                                                            PLAN !

Fig 4.5 Carrying out a measured building survey

44

(often filling a garage or two). see figs 4.6-4.8 – give guidance on space allowances.

STEP FOUR

Now you can bring steps one to three together. For a new home, your objective is to bring together the design concepts in your bubble or sketch doodle diagram (step one), to consider the allocation of space for movement, furniture and storage (step three) and to use the site survey which you will have set out on a grid (step two). Figure 4.8 shows typical sizes of homes in relation to the overall size and numbers of bedrooms. Use this as an early check to see the relative size of a new home in relation to the plot size available. You might conclude that what you're trying to build is just too big for the plot.

Another important aspect of developing the design at this stage is an appreciation of site characteristics (see Chapter 2). I find it valuable to plot these on my site survey. For example, record the prevailing wind direction, the source of any major noise (nearby road or airfield) and the best views out from the site. It's also worth recording any parts of the site affected by overlooking, trees and existing vegetation and the path of the sun from sunrise to sunset (see Figure 4.1 & 4.4). With a new home or an extension, you're trying to get an appreciation of overall size in terms

of numbers of bedrooms, numbers of reception rooms and very approximate sizes of these rooms. Here I find it helpful to cut out templates of the room sizes in thin card which I place on the site survey according to their best positions. For example, maybe you want the lounge to have the best views out of the site or to have the kitchen facing the entrance or driveway. Get an idea of how large the house needs to be from this process of checking the various constraints, including the size of site, your initial concept and needs for furniture, storage and circulation (see Figure 4.9 on Page 50).

If you're altering an existing building, the sequence is similar. Take the bubble diagram (step one) and, considering those requirements, allocate space using the information from step three. All this can then be plotted on the building survey grid (step two). Figure 4.5 shows this process using your 1:50 grid. The advantage of using tracing or see-through paper is that you can place it over a template representing furniture size. Alternatively, you can cut out shapes to represent the plan of furniture and then lay them on your survey grid. I find this an invaluable process in appreciating the space required to accommodate certain furniture or functions. Adding door swings helps your appreciation of circulation space. Always

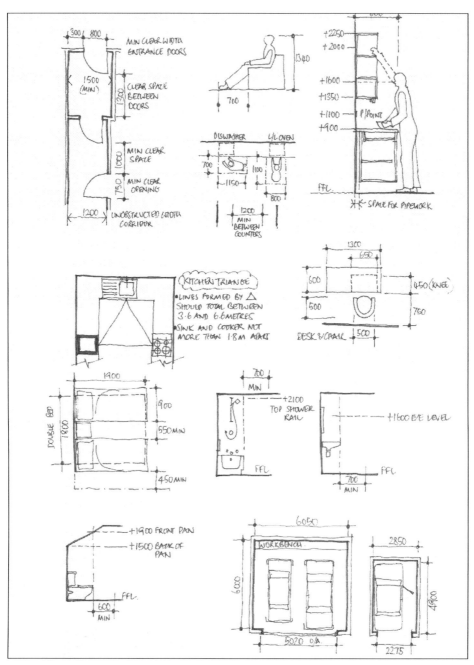

Fig 4.6 Space requirements... in your home

ADDITIONAL NOTES IN RELATION TO Fig 4.6 – SPACE FOR STORAGE IN YOUR HOME

1   Typical bedroom storage requirements for 2 people living together
    a) Ref. illustration 4.5. This shows an allowance of 900mm length of cupboard space for a man and 1.4m length for a woman. I suggest you allow a greater allowance and add a metre to each of these giving 2m storage for a man and 2.5m for a woman! If you are designing your new home you have an opportunity to create this sort of space for storage / clothes hanging. There are also excellent storage and cupboard sub-division systems now available so the space can be maximised.

2   Bathroom storage. Consider the following items: toilet rolls, soap, shampoos, spare toothpastes, lockable medicine cupboard. If you have the opportunity to have a large bathroom then have you considered putting a washing machine in the bathroom? (It is where you take your clothes off!)

3   Hall cupboards. You usually need 2 cupboards; one for storing domestic cleaning appliances and products; the other for coats, boots etc. It is often possible with a larger WC facility to accommodate coats within the WC. Think of the following items: coats, brollies, golf clubs, shoes, boots, cleaning equipment, hoover or vacuum cleaner, brooms, dustpan and brush.

4   Useful tips for storage and space saving techniques:
    a) Fitted bathroom furniture systems, vanity units with storage underneath, boxing in to enclose cisterns, all pipework can often be used for storage, under stair cupboards.
    b) Sometimes there is space available above stairs where the 2m headroom is not required; this is obviously got to be accessed from a first floor bedroom. Remember a roof window will give you extra headroom of around 250mm - 300mm below the actual roof window.
    c) Don't fill cupboards with hot water cylinders; consider a pressurised system allowing hot water cylinder to go in the roof or in less useable space.

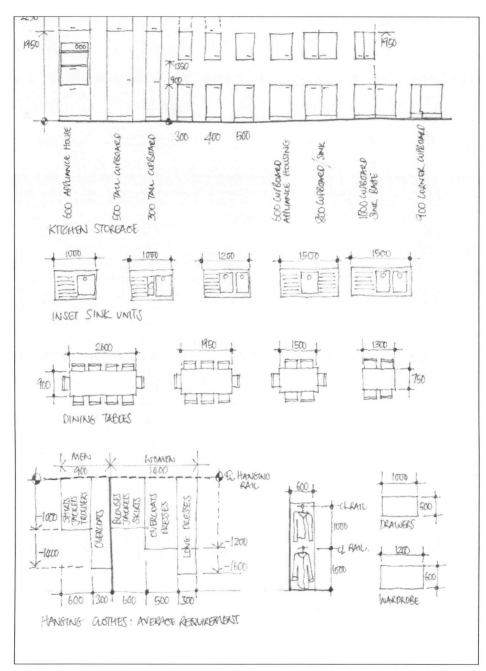

Fig 4.7 Space storage... in your home

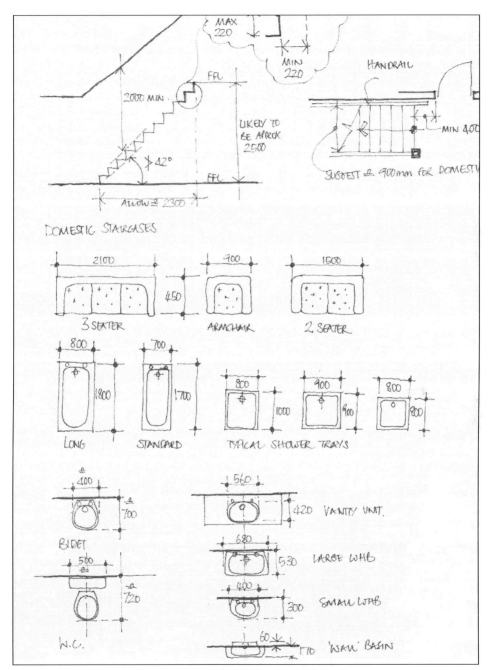

Fig 4.8 Space & storage ... in your home

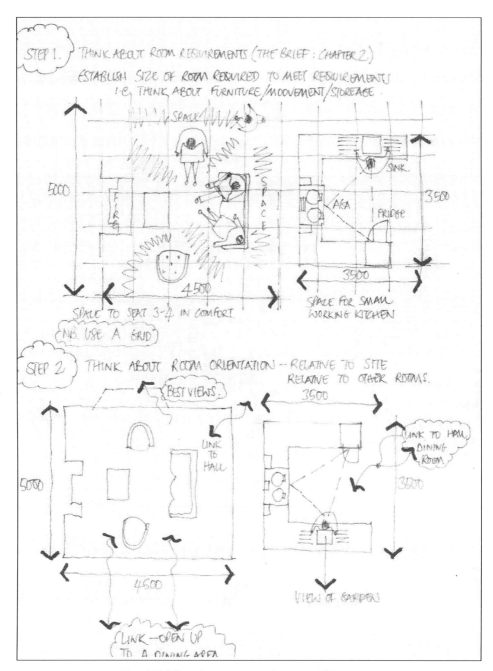

Fig 4.9 Thinking about space requirements within a room

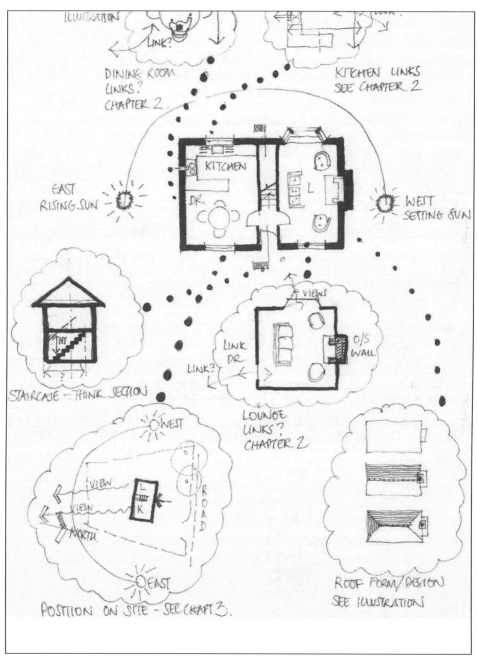

ILLUSTRATION

LINK?

DINING ROOM
LINKS?
CHAPTER 2.

KITCHEN LINKS
SEE CHAPTER 2

KITCHEN

DR.

EAST
RISING SUN

WEST
SETTING SUN

STAIRCASE - THINK SECTION

VIEWS

LINK
DR

O/S
WALL

LINK?

LOUNGE
LINKS?
CHAPTER 2

WEST

VIEW

VIEW

NORTH

L
K

R
O
A
D

EAST

POSITION ON SITE - SEE CHAPT 3.

ROOF FORM / DESIGN
SEE ILLUSTRATION

Fig 4.10 Thought processes... through the design

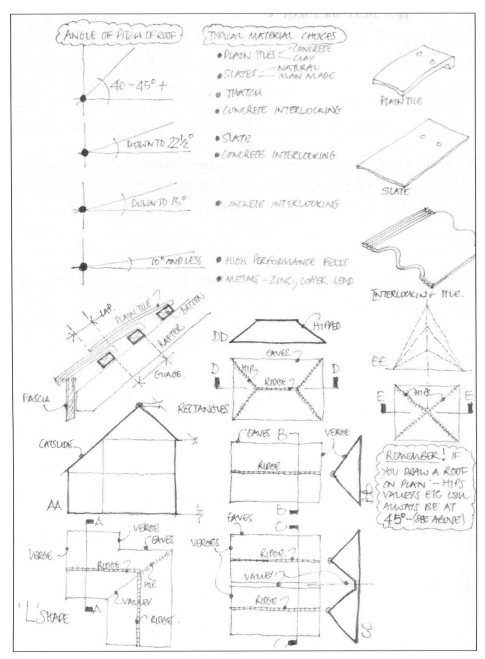

Fig 4.11 Roof arrangements

be realistic about where rooms should be to maximise on good views and garden aspect, for example, don't feel you have to have your kitchen at the front of the house just because it's always been there. At this stage, don't worry too much by technical requirements, drainage and other services.

By the end of step four you should be getting a much better understanding of the size of new home or extension you're likely to need to accommodate your requirements. You'll have a better appreciation of the space relative to the site area available and you'll be more focused on the constraints of your site. If you're altering an existing home, the 1:50 survey grid will have allowed you to consider alternative layouts.

STEP FIVE

In this step you draw a cross-section through your existing home, extension or site for a new build. In home building there are normally two types of section: one taken through a building or rooms; the other taken right through the ground that makes up the site. Figure 4.3 illustrates a building or room section. A room section is normally drawn at 1:20 scale and allows you to look into a particular room to understand the relative heights of floors, doors and ceilings. It's also a useful interior

decorating tool as you can colour up the section and see the effect of different decorative techniques or ideas. Building sections are drawn at a smaller scale and encompass the whole building. It's often used for understanding construction but we won't get into that at this stage. It does, however, give us an early indication of the bulk of a new extension relative to the existing building, which might well be important for obtaining planning permission (see Chapter 11). A site section is invaluable in showing the effect of new build or an extension in relation to adjacent buildings or surrounding features. In order to make a site section meaningful, it's necessary to plot approximate ground levels.

STEP SIX

This stage is about building form (the shape of the building), materials and construction type. A building form might be emerging already from the work you've done so far - it could be long and thin, rectangular or one of a variety of other shapes. Now's the time to think about how such a building shape might be roofed over. Figure 4.11 illustrates common traditional roof arrangements used in home building. When viewed on plan roof lines are always drawn at 45°, no matter what the pitch really is. (It took me a number of years to

Fig 4.12 The two photos on this page are the pre-building models...

...and these two photographs are of the real thing!

Fig 4.13 The use of models can be really helpful in understanding the design

realise this simple point!). The pitch or steepness of the roof determines the type of roof covering material you can use and Figure 4.11 gives examples of materials used at different pitches.

Local building styles often influence the type of materials used for new buildings. Whether I'm designing a new home or extending an existing one, I spend a lot of time in the area absorbing the nature of local buildings. I'll usually spend an hour or two driving around an area taking photographs of materials and details. We'll look at construction types later (Chapter 7) but

normally at this point I review the basic options available for house building. When you've got to this stage in the design process, it's often beneficial to construct a three-dimensional model of your design. There are various options - you can use a simple computer aided design (CAD) programme (such as AutoCAD Light) or you can build a simple cardboard model. I often make simple card models.

STEP SEVEN

Now you get down to design style and design detail. Figure 4.15 shows two scenarios, one with the same building with different styles and the same building with and without building detail. Design style is often a matter of personal preference although in order to obtain planning permission one is often steered in the direction of using traditional building styles. Design details, as the illustration shows, are the ears, mouth, eyes of a building and, in my view, are incredibly important.

STEP EIGHT

Refers to other chapters and to the use of computer software. My view of computer software is that it can be extremely helpful once you have established your brief and gone through the exercises described in Chapter 4. It is only by making yourself totally aware of all the design constraints that you can then use computer software much more effectively.

Fig 4.14 Modern link between two older buildings

CHAPTER 5

DESIGN STYLES

In this chapter I share with you some of my ideas on how to select a building style, whether you're building your new home, extending an existing one or giving your present home a complete facelift or transformation to a different style. Listed below is the historical sequence of widely recognised building styles.

■ Tudor and Jacobean 1485 – 1625

■ Baroque 1625 – 1714

■ Early Georgian 1714 – 1765

■ Colonial 1667 – 1780

■ Late Georgian 1765 – 1811

■ Regency & early 19th century 1811 –1837

■ British Victorian 1837 – 1901

■ Arts and Crafts 1860 – 1925

■ Art Nouveau 1888 – 1905

■ Edwardian 1901 – 1914

■ Twenties and Thirties: the Modern Movement 1920 – 1950

■ Beyond modern 1920 – 1996

I've grouped the various historical periods set out above into three main design-style periods commonly used for new homes:

■ early years, including mediaeval architecture

■ middle years, from early Georgian to 19th century

■ later years, incorporating Victorian, Edwardian, Arts and Crafts and contemporary style from late 20th century up to the present day

Design style is usually influenced by the era in which the house was designed, the economic conditions, the location, fashions and influences from abroad. Many houses are a wonderful mix of styles, comprising various building characteristics, such as window and door size, frequency, proportion, materials and the way in which the structure is put together. In designing a house, you have a unique opportunity to select your building style. But, before explaining how to do this, here's my list of frequently asked questions about building styles.

CAN I MIX DESIGN STYLES IN MY HOME?

Yes. Many inspirational ideas come from the past and few ideas are truly innovative. I often commission archaeological surveys when I'm working on historic buildings and am amazed by the way historic houses evolve over many hundreds of years, incorporating a mix of styles, ideas and treatments.

IS IT WRONG TO COPY STYLES AND DETAILS?

I don't think so (providing you don't breach copyright, of course). You should be like a camera recording ideas and building details in your mind all the time so you can use them later in the design of your new home or extension. Good designs are sensitive to their surroundings.

It's the way building details are used that determines whether a design is successful.

WHAT STYLE SHOULD WE USE FOR OUR NEW HOME OR EXTENSION?

These suggestions should help you decide:

■ Understand fully your requirements. A particular style might suit the way you want to live. For example, I've on occasion questioned whether a 15th or 16th century cottage style, where space can be very limited, would be suitable for a family of six growing children. Here, again, is the need to think ahead.

■ Study the locality. Take time to study the environment and existing houses in the area and make notes about styles, proportions, materials and details or, what is often termed, the 'local vernacular'. This could lead you to a particular design style.

■ Be aware of site pressures. These can include views, prevailing weather, sun path and orientation. Style can often evolve from such factors. For example, if you're building a new home on a site with spectacular views, this might prompt you to design in a more contemporary style that allows large areas of glass to make the most of the views.

■ Take account of construction cost. When constructing a new home or extension, the more complex the building, generally the greater the cost. This is covered in greater depth in Chapter 10. For example, if you try to reproduce an oak frame building with exposed timbers externally and internally, it'll be more expensive than a simpler construction method. Later on during the 20th century, styles like the Arts and Crafts movement (see below) involved complex building shape and detailing which inevitably adds to cost. If you're working on a historic building it might be listed (the government lists buildings with architectural or historic interest and this restricts how the building can be extended or altered (see Chapter 11).

IS SALEABILITY AFFECTED BY DESIGN STYLE?

In my experience, building design is highly influential and can significantly affect saleability. A really well designed home, which respects a particular design style and is well executed and nicely finished, makes for an easier sale. Home owners are becoming more discerning and are looking to achieve higher standards of design (read the design style characteristics below carefully).

SHOULD AN EXTENSION COPY THE DESIGN STYLE OF MY EXISTING HOME?

There are two schools of thought: one is to emulate the style of the existing building; the other is to build an extension that contrasts with the existing home. It's probably more difficult to build a successfully designed extension in a contrasting style. If you build to match the existing building, the extension should have a seamless joint with the existing structure and be respectful. This usually means being subservient, or at a smaller scale, to the existing house, though there are obviously exceptions to this. Remember the passage of time - if you choose a currently fashionable building design style, consider what it would look like in the longer term and how it would affect the sale of your home in five or ten years time.

Now let's look at the characteristics, advantages and disadvantages of using a particular style in the construction of your new home, extension or alteration.

EARLY YEARS

This incorporates styles from 15th century, including mediaeval styles, to Tudor, Jacobean and Elizabethan styles (about 1485 – 1625). See fig 5.2

WHAT IT LOOKS LIKE/ CHARACTERISTICS:

When you are considering a design style for your new home, remember to spend time looking around locally at examples of the period that you are interested in. Note the characteristics and use of materials. The early years of home

FIG 5.1 MAIN CHARACTERISTICS OF DESIGN STYLES

BUILDING DETAIL / FEATURE PREFERRED	LIKELY BUILDING STYLE
COLUMNS & BRACKETING	MEDIAEVAL / CONTEMPORARY
INGLENOOK FIREPLACE	MEDIAEVAL
BEAMED CEILINGS ALL EXPOSED	MEDIAEVAL
COVING, PLASTER MOULDINGS, DADO RAILS ETC.	GEORGIAN
LEADED LIGHT WINDOWS	GOTHIC
RECTANGULAR BAY WINDOWS	MEDIAEVAL / GEORGIAN
CANTILEVERED FIRST FLOORS	MEDIAEVAL / CONTEMPORARY
EXPOSED STRUCTURAL COLUMNS INSIDE	MEDIAEVAL / CONTEMPORARY
TIMBER MOULDINGS, DADO	GEORGIAN / EDWARDIAN
TIMBER PANELLING PAINTED	VICTORIAN / EDWARDIAN
WOOD	GEORGIAN / CONTEMPORARY
WIDE ELEGANT OPEN STAIRCASES	GEORGIAN / CONTEMPORARY
IRON RAILINGS	GEORGIAN / CONTEMPORARY
CASEMENT WINDOWS	ALL STYLES
SLIDING SASH WINDOWS	GEORGIAN / EDWARDIAN / VICTORIAN
SPIRAL STAIRCASE	CONTEMPORARY
GALLERIED LANDINGS	MEDIAEVAL / CONTEMPORARY
BRIGHT AIRY ENVIRONMENT WITH HIGH CEILINGS	GEORGIAN / CONTEMPORARY
COSY, SNUG LOW CEILINGS	MEDIAEVAL / CONTEMPORARY
BAY WINDOWS, CIRCULAR	GEORGIAN / CONTEMPORARY
ORIEL WINDOWS	
FLOOR TO CEILING GLAZING	CONTEMPORARY
SLIDING FOLDING DOORS	CONTEMPORARY
BASEMENTS	CONTEMPORARY
SUNKEN BATHS	CONTEMPORARY
USE OF OAK	MEDIAEVAL / CONTEMPORARY
LARGE FLOOR TO CEILING WINDOWS	CONTEMPORARY
CURVED & CIRCULAR BUILDING FORMS	CONTEMPORARY
RICH DETAIL, POINTED WINDOW HEADS	GOTHIC / VICTORIAN REVIVAL
CIRCULAR / ARCHED WINDOW HEADS	GOTHIC / VICTORIAN REVIVAL

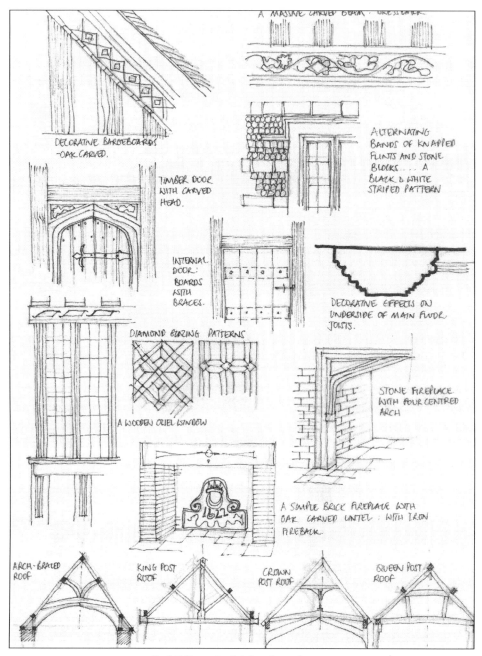

Fig 5.2 Elements of style... the early years

building are often going to demonstrate the use of local materials. For example, in the south east there is going to be a lot of timber, usually oak, with exposed oak frames. Later in the early years period you will see examples of brick and clay tiles. Early buildings will also tend to have small windows and steep pitched roofs. As you move around the country you will see different examples of construction materials such as local stone instead of timber used in walling materials.

Looking at examples of the early years buildings remember also that they will have been adapted and altered often over many hundreds of years so what you are looking at can be a mix of different design styles. For example, in Sussex you will find an original oak framed building has often been replaced with brick at the ground floor level as the frame has deteriorated over many hundreds of years.

ROOFS:

Building a new home or extension often provides an opportunity to expose the roof structure internally. Figure 5.2 shows different types of roof structure and how to create a really dramatic interior. Exposed roof structures can work well in a bedroom or hall, which looks up two storeys internally. Externally, roofs from this period have many interesting features including carved timber fascias, especially to the gables, and exposed rafter feet (see Figure 5.3). If you're in an area that uses thatch it's worth considering that roof form. Otherwise, the most likely roof coverings are plain clay tiles or perhaps 'stone slates'. Go for quality roofing materials, using the real thing rather than imitations.

WALLS:

A green oak timber frame was often used in this period. This construction gives you rendered panels. If you're using solid masonry construction, don't miss the opportunity to mix materials. As an example, stone blocks and napped flints. The character of timber frame varies between different areas. In the midlands and the north you could consider a cruck frame, which would introduce some dramatic effects. Walls are often jettied or cantilevered out at first floor level, externally, exposing floor joists or finishing them off with Bressimer type beams, which were often carved (see Figure 5.1).

FLOORS AND FINISHES:

Flagstones probably look most appropriate with the inside of a timber frame. Rush matting also looks good.

Brick chimneys: These often have octagonal shafts and involve the use of special or rubbed bricks (see Figure 5.3).

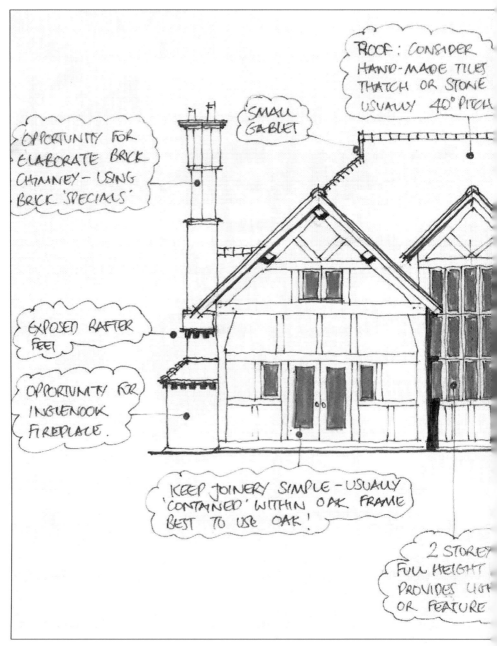

ROOF: CONSIDER
HAND-MADE TILES
THATCH OR STONE
USUALLY 40° PITCH

SMALL
GABLET

OPPORTUNITY FOR
ELABORATE BRICK
CHIMNEY - USING
BRICK 'SPECIALS'

EXPOSED RAFTER
FEET

OPPORTUNITY FOR
INGLENOOK
FIREPLACE.

KEEP JOINERY SIMPLE - USUALLY
'CONTAINED' WITHIN OAK FRAME
BEST TO USE OAK!

2 STOREY
FULL HEIGHT
PROVIDES LIGHT
OR FEATURE

Fig 5.3 Character

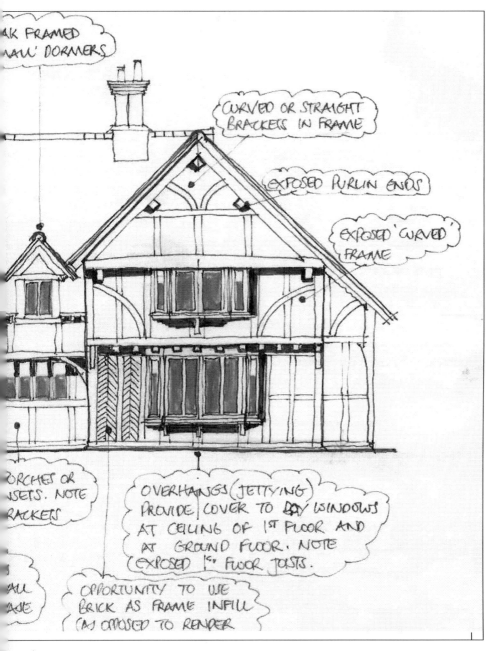

AK FRAMED
'WALL' DORMERS

CURVED OR STRAIGHT
BRACKETS IN FRAME

EXPOSED PURLIN ENDS

EXPOSED 'CURVED'
FRAME

ORCHES OR
JSETS. NOTE
RACKETS

OVERHANGS (JETTYING)
PROVIDE COVER TO BAY WINDOWS
AT CEILING OF 1ST FLOOR AND
AT GROUND FLOOR. NOTE
EXPOSED 1ST FLOOR JOISTS.

OPPORTUNITY TO USE
BRICK AS FRAME INFILL
(AS OPPOSED TO RENDER

J
ALL
ASE

...e early years

65

Be careful if building an inglenook (large fireplace recess), as the proportion of the opening needs to be worked out in relation to the cross-sectional area of the flue. The key is to make sure the fireplace enclosure (although located in a large recess) is enclosed to prevent it smoking.

DOORS:

Externally and internally you can increase importance of door openings by forming simple canopies or ornamental arched heads. Ironmongery (strap hinges and metal latches) for this period is readily available and it's worth shopping around. Internal doors are often simply boards fixed together usually with five horizontal members and installed within the oak frame with no linings, stops or architraves (see Figure 5.3).

WINDOWS:

Don't forget the way in which mullions and jambs (window timbers) were moulded. Windows were often small, with small spaces between mullions. Stone window surrounds can be totally in keeping where you're building in masonry. This era used many different styles and patterns of glazing (see Figures 5.2 and 5.3).

CEILINGS:

During the early years ceilings were really the underside of the floor above. If your design draws on the early period, they could just be simple exposed joists and beams. The later stages of this period would have seen carving to the underside of beams.

ADVANTAGES:

Houses based on early years designs are generally appealing and a very saleable style which creates a cosy atmosphere full of character.

DISADVANTAGES:

This style is expensive to construct, not only in the structure but also in the finishes. Generally it's fairly high maintenance the more authentic the building is made to look. Remember, if you're altering an existing building the following areas might represent an uphill battle:

■ draughts and air leakage

■ poor insulation, difficult to keep warm

■ generally lack of storage space, our home requirements are greatly different to what they were in the early years

■ dampness, both rising and penetrating

■ integrating modern services, there are few voids and space will be at a premium

■ genuinely historic buildings are almost certainly going to be listed and there'll be restrictions on what you can do and how it's done (see Chapter 11)

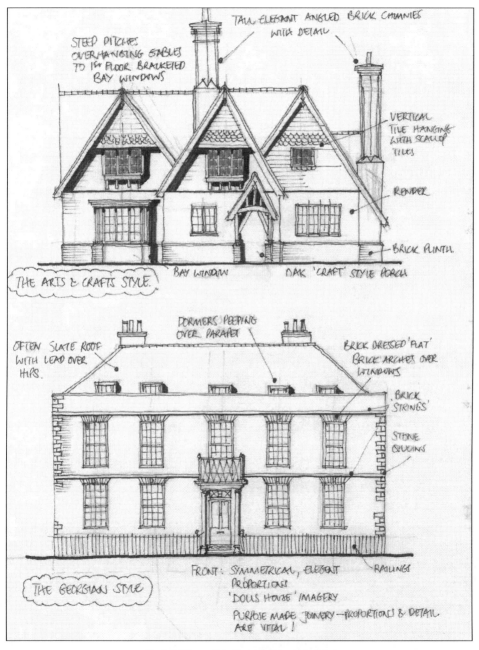

STEEP PITCHES
OVERHANGING GABLES
TO 1ST FLOOR BRACKETED
BAY WINDOWS

TALL ELEGANT ANGLED BRICK CHIMNIES
WITH DETAIL

VERTICAL
TILE HANGING
WITH SCALLOP
TILES

RENDER

BRICK PLINTH.

BAY WINDOW

OAK 'CRAFT' STYLE PORCH

THE ARTS & CRAFTS STYLE.

DORMERS PEEPING
OVER PARAPET

OFTEN SLATE ROOF
WITH LEAD OVER
HIPS.

BRICK DRESSED 'FLAT'
BRICK ARCHES OVER
WINDOWS

'BRICK
STRINGS'

STONE
QUOINS

RAILINGS

THE GEORGIAN STYLE

FRONT: SYMMETRICAL, ELEGANT
PROPORTIONS
'DOLLS HOUSE' IMAGERY

PURPOSE MADE JOINERY — PROPORTIONS & DETAIL
ARE VITAL!

Fig 5.4 Arts and Crafts and Georgian styles

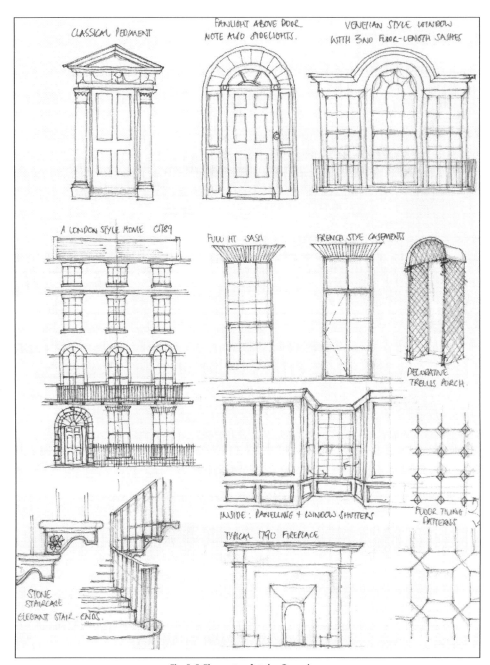

Fig 5.5 Elements of style: Georgian

MIDDLE YEARS

This includes early to late Georgian, Regency and early 18th to mid-19th century.

What it looks like/characteristics: These designs have simple rectangular plan forms, elegant proportions, plain brick gauged arches, elegant entry doors and parapet walls, behind which there are often hipped and low pitch roofs. The style is all about light and elegance. Design details often incorporate cupolas, quoins, dormers, big sash windows, sometimes full height (through which you can actually walk), wrought ironwork, rooms panelled in wood or plaster, elegant fireplaces, high ceilings, balconies, low window cills, door encasements and elegant staircases (see fig 5.5). Middle years properties often lend themselves to terraced homes.

DOORS:

The front entrance was always an important part of the design. It was usually a plain door (a six-panel door often looks best) with elaborate surrounds (see Figure 5.4). Glazed fanlights and sidelights can be a great way of introducing light into the hall of a new home. Internal doors typically would be six-panelled with large architraves, carvings and classical details surrounding the doors. No design would be complete without some stylish door furniture (see Figure 5.5).

WINDOWS:

Figure 5.5 shows typical window proportions for a Georgian terraced house. On the first floor it's common to have low sills opening onto balconies. Windows can be big sashes or French doors to let people out onto the balcony.

WALLS:

In your new home think about cladding the walls of your important reception rooms in timber panelling which was typical of the period (see figure 5.6). When forming openings between rooms, look carefully at the way the style took time and trouble to detail the door surround. See that the door frame becomes an integral part of the surround to the door with careful detailing of architrave and how this joins up with the panelling. With an important opening, consider the opportunity of using an arch.

CEILINGS:

These can vary from simple to very elaborate. There's an enormous range of covings, dados, skirtings and ceiling mouldings you can incorporate if you're building from scratch. The more elaborate and larger the room the more elaborate the detail can be.

FLOORS:

Appropriate materials are flagstones

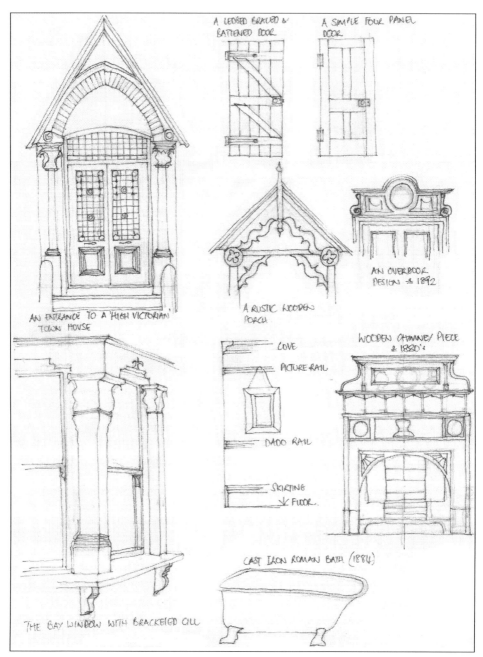

Fig 5.6 Elements of style: Victorian and Edwardian

or elegant stone tiling on the ground floor, with wide oak boarding on upper floors. The Georgian period often used stone with black diamond patterns at the intersections (see Figure 5.5). There might be an opportunity in an entrance hall to pick up the pattern generated by a staircase gallery or a roof light, which is typical of this style.

FIREPLACES:

These were a social focal point, with surrounds often constructed in marble and wood. There are many options available to you in refurbishment or buying new.

STAIRCASES:

The Georgian staircase can be a wonderfully elegant feature typically featuring sweeping handrails and bullnose treads. If you have the funds, a stone staircase with a steel balustrade can look very dramatic (see Figure 5.5).

BUILT-IN FURNITURE:

This period was the first to utilise built-in furniture and you can take the opportunity in designing a new home or alterations to incorporate dining room cupboards or library book cases. Built-in cupboards can be 'doored' to match the interior of the room, for example, using 6-panel doors and all cupboards

or niches can be coordinated with panelling.

LIGHTING:

Traditionally, this period would have used chandeliers. Fortunately, we have much better lighting technology now (see Chapter 9). However, a chandelier in a reception room still provides an important focal point in the centre of the ceiling of the room. Outside, you can think about including lighting in railings. This period featured metal railings, gates, balconies and all these elements are available to you as a home designer, especially if you're building anew.

ADVANTAGES:

This style gives you the opportunity to create elegance, proportion, space, light and airiness. In a new home it allows you to incorporate balconies, sweeping elegant staircase, fireplace, built-in furniture and many other features. Make use of under floor heating, as there aren't any Georgian style radiators.

DISADVANTAGES:

Because of the proportions, this style tends to cost more as volumes are generally greater. Bear in mind homes in this style don't lend themselves to clutter.

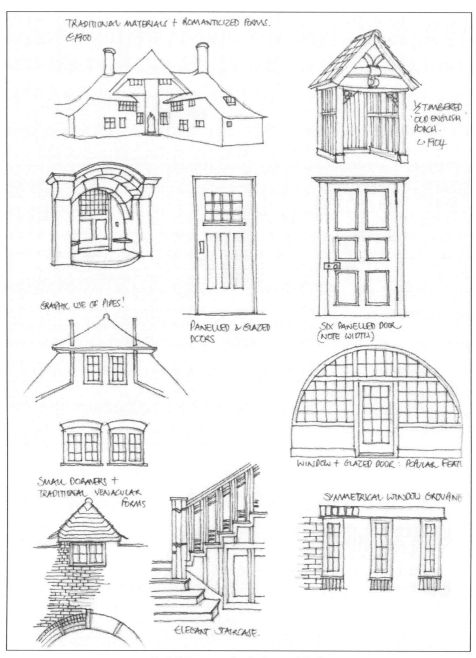

Fig 5.7 Elements of style: Arts and Crafts

LATER YEARS

This covers Victorian, Arts and Crafts, Art Nouveau, Edwardian to mid 20th century. The period is, in my view, a wonderful 'library' for building detail as it draws upon the earlier styles, adapts and develops them so that they are more sophisticated and, in some cases, more refined.

VICTORIAN

One third of the houses in Britain date from the Victorian period so, if you're refurbishing an existing home, it's highly likely it'll be Victorian.

What it looks like/characteristics: Victorian was really a revival from the past. It used mock Gothic-style, Greek revival, Romanesque, Tudor Elizabethan and Italianate. It's typified by half-timbered gables, classic sash windows, red brick terracotta ornament and elaborate porches.

PORCHES:

If you're building a Victorian-style home, you need to have an elaborate porch - the bigger the house, the more elaborate the porch. In a terrace there are often opportunities to recess a porch, which can have an equally imposing impact (see Figure 5.6).

Internal doors: Figure 5.6 includes some typical Victorian-style doors. A four-panel door is probably the most common with moulding around the four panels being an important feature. This can lift the door and make it much more interesting and of higher quality. The Victorian style often used 'over-doors', which are really details in painted timber above the actual door. Borrowed lights were also typical of this period.

WINDOWS:

A Victorian home must have a bay window. This can either be supported on brackets or taken down to a foundation. Stained glass to stair and landing widows was a feature of the period. See Figure 5.6 for typical window styles.

INTERNAL WALLS:

These were usually divided into three: from floor to a dado moulding (chair height); from dado to a picture rail moulding; and from picture rail to ceiling level, often including a cornice (see Figure 5.6). Wallpapers were common in Victorian times, anaglypta, for example. Panelling was common in halls and studies, either oak or pine. In a new home, why not panel one room?

FLOORS:

Different coloured clay tiling was used especially in entrance halls and conservatories. (This was often referred to as encaustic tiling – 'burnt in'). Parquet floors were also frequently used. These materials are now readily available for use in refurbishment or building a new home

FIREPLACE:

The fireplace was an essential focal point in a Victorian home. Think about buying a wooden chimney piece, which would have often been painted (see Figure 5.6).

STAIRCASES:

These were an important feature. If they were stone, they usually had cast iron balustrades. Polished hardwood spindles were used in wooden staircases. One widespread Victorian feature worth considering is a stencilled design on the wall between the string of the stair and dado rail as the stair rises.

BUILT-IN FURNITURE:

This was regularly included and in a new Victorian-style home my advice is to go for it. Typically, in a bedroom you can incorporate cupboards, dressing table and seats - all very Victorian. Built-in seats around a fireplace in the sitting room was characteristic of this style.

SANITARYWARE:

Many companies specialise in providing Victorian-style sanitary ware. The typical free-standing cast iron bath will have a

dramatic effect on the way you lay out a bathroom.

EXTERNAL:

Look at how the Victorians used lighting, metalwork and woodwork, pioneering decorative bargeboards and conservatories. Victorian design conservatories are widely available and can fit in beautifully with an existing home of that time or a new Victorian-style one.

ARTS AND CRAFTS

If this style interests you, take the opportunity to research people such as William Morris, Edwin Lutyens and Charles Voysey, who were important names during this architectural period. It was all to do with honesty of material and craftsmanship.

WHAT IT LOOKS LIKE/ CHARACTERISTICS

The Arts and Crafts Movement utilised traditional materials with romanticised forms.

DOORS

The emphasis was on width, panelling and glazing (see Figure 5.7).

PORCHES

Often dramatic, these may give a

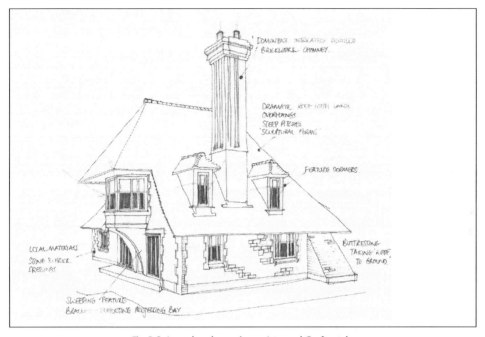

Fig 5.8 A modern home in an Arts and Crafts style

sympathetic nod to earlier styles (see Figure 5.7).

WINDOWS

Great oriel windows are appropriate if you're building a new home, as are symmetrical windows, small dormer windows, windows in groups (see Figure 5.7).

WALLS:

Walls would often be clad inside with panelling with elaborate borders along the top of the panelling before going into wallpaper, a picture rail and a painted ceiling. Panelling would either be natural wood and quite often painted white or even a bold colour

CEILINGS:

Used stencilled patterns, barrel vaulting, exposed beams (back to vernacular).

Built-in furniture was, as with the Victorian period, popular in the Arts & Crafts Movement.

ADVANTAGES:

Style provides homes with rich internal comfortable derails characterised by elaborate fireplaces, niches, warm and liveable style creating a lovely family home. This style has bought together with of the advantages of the earlier architectural styles and has a lot to offer in modern home design (see fig 5.8).

DISADVANTAGES:

Because of the rich detailing, it can be an expensive style to recreate.

CONTEMPORARY
(THIS RUNS FROM LATE 20TH THROUGH TO THE 21ST CENTURY)

WHAT IT LOOKS LIKE/ CHARACTERISTICS

Contemporary exhibits clean, sculptural lines and steel and glass are often used. It features canopies, crisp edges and plain woodwork, avoiding traditional joinery detail such as skirtings and architraves. Construction lends itself to prefabrication; tolerances are more precise and, therefore, different to previous building systems. This sort of construction / detailing lends itself to prefabrication. In earlier architectural styles, much of the work was done on site. Because of the simplified detailing and small tolerances, this style lends itself to pre-fabrication.

ROOFS:

The contemporary style roof is characterised by its simplicity and clean sharp lines. They will often be low or flat pitched roofs behind parapets. Metal roofs are often used and you will see copper and zinc characterised by their different colours and the way they are detailed / finished off.

FLOORS AND FLOOR FINISHES:

 Large format stone tiling, precise jointing often without any form of skirting.

DOORS:

A simple detailing with quality ironmongery.

WINDOWS:

Metal windows are common with minimal frames and large areas of glazing. Contemporary style will push glazing technology to its limits in term of natural and solar control glasses.

CHIMNEYS

Chimneys will often be sculptural forms, they could even use stainless steel flues.

ADVANTAGES:

This style can look magnificent. Light, airy spaces, clean lines, a fresh airy living style. It requires a disciplined lifestyle to avoid clutter.

DISADVANTAGES:

Question how it'll look in five to ten years' time. These styles don't lend themselves

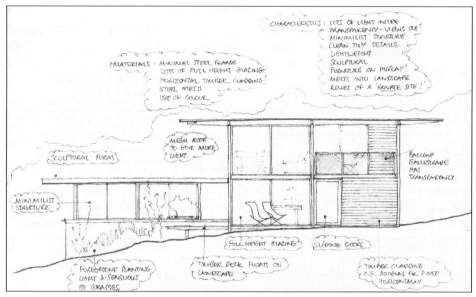

fig 5.9 A contemporary style home

to family clutter. Although they might look simple, they are usually extremely expensive to do properly.

ECO-HOME

What it looks like/characteristics: This type of home is often based on a timber frame, with large south-facing windows and small north-facing windows, perhaps incorporating a conservatory as a heat store. The specification of an environmentally-friendly house produces a style that appears not to relate to anything previously seen. Such houses tend to have a modern feel because of the use of particular materials. (see fig 5.10 on next page)

WALLS:

You will often see thick external walling to help create thermal mass. This allows heating systems to use the walling as a thermal store heating it up and then releasing the heat slowly over a period of time. You will see the use of local materials of low embodied energy, i.e. materials which do not need enormous amounts of energy to produce or transport to the site. Walls will also be very carefully detailed where they join ceilings and walls to prevent air leakage. This all helps to avoid unnecessary energy losses as a result of a building leaking or suffering from draughts.

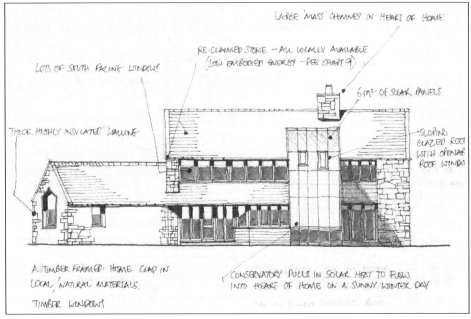

Fig 5.10 An 'Eco' home

FLOORS AND FLOOR FINISHES:

Large format stone tiling, precise jointing often without any form of skirting.

WINDOWS / PORCHES ETC:

An Eco home will often incorporate large areas of south facing glazing and even a conservatory type sunroom to create a buffer between living spaces and the outside air. This creates a sort of inside/outside space which is kept warm throughout the year as a result of solar gain.

BASEMENTS:

You may also find that an Eco home makes use of space below a house with a basement. This has zero impact on the environment as it is usually invisible, it will have virtually zero energy losses. Sustainability is the buzz word for eco homes so siting and hi-tech appliances such as grey water recycling, ground source heat pumps, high efficiency boilers, underfloor heating and sophisticated control systems all characterise the Eco home. More information can be seen in later Chapters.

ADVANTAGES:

They are, by design, very energy efficient

with low-environmental impact and very low maintenance costs.

DISADVANTAGES:

Eco-homes can be expensive to construct. In the short term, eco-homes might not be as saleable as the more traditional styles – a situation I envisage changing as this form of building becomes more popular.

CHAPTER 6
DESIGN DETAILS

This chapter sets out some of the design details which will make up your new home, extension or alteration and others which can be used transform your design from the ordinary to the exceptional. Look through the various headings and illustrations to stimulate your imagination to see the options you have. For example, if you're constructing your new home out of brickwork, have you considered using a brick plinth where the brickwork meets the ground? What about a corbelled eaves detail to add interest where the wall joins the roof overhang.

EXTERNAL WALLS
This refers to the external skin or outside face of the external construction (construction is covered in Chapter 7).

CONSTRUCTION
Check out your local area to see how walls are detailed. Ask your builder to make up a small sample panel so you can judge walling materials such as brick, stone, render, flint before you go ahead and construct the real thing. In considering wall design, transitions are important - between wall and ground

and wall and roof, around openings and at corners (see below).

BRICK

There are hundreds of different bricks, mortars and mortar joints. Combinations of these options give all kinds of weathering effects and different aesthetics. Look around at existing brickwork locally and find out the local type of brick used. Notice the way the mortar has been finished off. Take photographs and show your home designer what you like. Builders' merchants are good places to look to see sample panels of different brickwork.

STONE

Again, there are numerous types of stone and different finishes to it. One feature to bear in mind is that stone can be finished or dressed so that it has a smooth or textured surface. Sizes of stone (random or regular sizes) greatly affect what a wall looks like (see fig 6.1).

FLINT

There are various methods of preparing and finishing flint. Flint can be knapped or cut in half, which gives a completely different effect to leaving it whole. If you're in an area where flint is used, look around to find and record a form of

construction you like (see fig 6.2).

RENDER

Sometimes referred to as stucco, this can come in many textures. The way the render is finished off around window and door openings is very important if it's going to be maintained in a pristine condition. The secret here is to make sure that water is shed from openings, so drips are important. Pre-coloured renders are available which means you don't have to paint them. Renders can be given various effects by the application of masonry paints to add interesting textures and colours. Don't forget that applied finishes usually need regular maintenance.

Tile hanging. This means using what are, in effect, roof tiles hung vertically on the walls. There's an enormous range of tiles available. Slates and cedar shingles can also be used in this way.

GLASS

You can use specially strengthened and supported glass in home design provided you take specialist advice. There are also control glasses, which can restrict the amount of heat coming in and out. You can even buy 'privalite' glass, which can be electrically switched on to make it obscure or turned off to make it clear.

TIMBER CLADDINGS

Horizontal weather-boarding (Figure 6.1) comes either in plain rectangular sections, feather edged, rebated feather edged or rebated and tongue and grooved, often referred to as shiplap. If you're planning to stain horizontal weatherboarding, it's generally better if it's rough sawn as the stain sinks into the timber better. Timber boarding can also be applied vertically. Cedar is a popular material that's relatively maintenance-free and fades to a

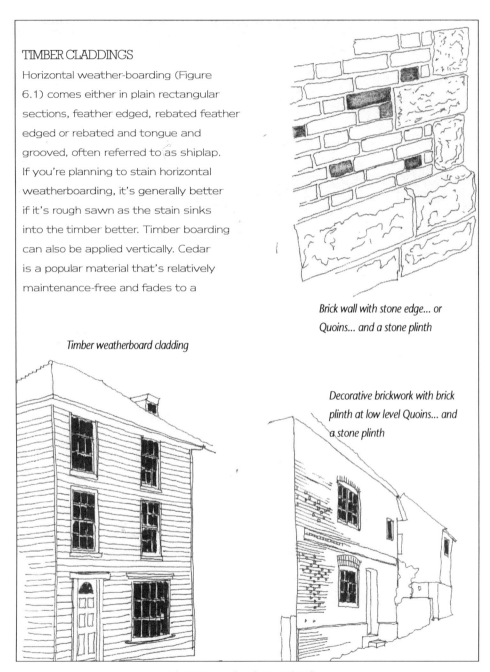

Brick wall with stone edge... or Quoins... and a stone plinth

Timber weatherboard cladding

Decorative brickwork with brick plinth at low level Quoins... and a stone plinth

Fig 6.1 Examples of external walls

TIMBER FRAME WALLING...

UNDRESSED STONE...

FLINT WITH BRICK DRESSINGS TO
WINDOW/DOORS

A JETTIED FIRST FLOOR

Fig 6.2 Examples of external walls

pleasant grey colour after a few years of exposure. Oak is a beautiful material and is maintenance-free; in time, it fades to a golden grey.

WALLS: DESIGN FEATURES

JETTYING

This means forming an overhang in the vertical surfaces of walls, one above another (see Figure 6.2). It's a mediaeval feature and can look really effective if the floor joists are cantilevered (projected) over a wall to support the wall above.

Plinths. These are often formed at low level around the base of a ground floor wall, usually when building in brick or stone. This gives a home a feeling that it's firmly positioned on the ground and adds interest to a wall that would otherwise simply run into the ground (see Figure 6.1).

BRICK DRESSINGS

The nature of materials like stone, flint or render are such that they're difficult to finish around window or door openings. One solution is to use a dressing (usually brick) to surround a window or door opening. Rendered dressings around window and door openings are commonly found in the north of England (see Figure 6.2).

ARCHES

There are many forms of arch found in home construction. They're usually formed in a masonry material such as brick or stone, cut and shaped (or dressed) to form an arch. An attractive feature I've used in period homes is the flat brick arch. Here brickwork is used as a horizontal beam over the head of a window or door. The bricks are cut and dressed to form what's called a flat arch.

BUTTRESSES

These are interesting features often used to provide strength to an old wall. I have used them in new home construction to create a heavy feel to a ground floor wall construction. They are usually constructed in brick and need care where the brick changes from a sloping plane to a vertical plane.

STRING COURSES

You'll see these incorporated in all types of wall construction. They comprise contrasting horizontal lines taken around an external wall simply to break it up and provide interest. They're formed in brick, render or even in stone. String courses are a nice feature and often under utilised in new home construction.

EAVES

Give some though to the way a wall

is finished off at high level before it meets the eaves of the roof. There are many fabulous examples of decorative brickwork usually corbelled (or stepped) out to make the transition between the top of the wall and the roof construction (see Figure 6.1). One of the more common eaves details is the dog tooth, where the brick steps in and out, the brick that steps out supports another brick which is corbelled out further to the eaves. It adds interest and detail and is an under used way of forming the transition between wall and roof planes. It also avoids the use of fascias supporting gutters, which need maintenance.

QUOINS

Quoins are the detail at wall corners (see Figure 6.1). Depending on the locality, they can be constructed in timber blocks, stone or brick. They add an interesting feature to an otherwise simple change of direction of the wall surface (see Figure 6.1).

WINDOWS

The two most common types of window are the sliding sash and casement (see Figures 6,2, 6.3 and 6.4). The sliding sash originates in the early Georgian period and is actually quite a complicated mechanism whereby one window slides vertically up inside or outside the other. It also has balancing weights so that it can be left partially open. In designing windows, you can make the glass panes any size and include glazing bars (criss-crosses of timber across the window sub-dividing the plane). The size of window and the way it is sub-divided has a big impact on how your house looks. Thick glazing bars, often used to support double glazing units, look heavy and unsightly when a widow is sub-divided by many glazing bars. Casement windows are any windows that are hinged on one side and open either inwards our outwards, as opposed to top hung (hinged at the top) or centre pivot (pivoting from its horizontal central axis).

Windows are the eyes of a building and you need to get the size, proportion and style right if your home design is going to look good. Ask your home designer to show you alternatives, not only in style but also in materials. Windows are either bought off-the-shelf (mass-produced) or purpose-made. If you have a historic building, it's desirable to get the windows purpose made and your home designer will need to put together precise details for a joiner to make them up. Window frames can be made in various materials - softwood, hardwood, metal, aluminium, plastic or a combination of materials. Each produces a different effect. Some manufacturers try to combine the weathering properties of maintenance-free materials, such as aluminium or plastic, externally, with the aesthetic qualities of wood, internally. The choices are enormous and I can't over emphasise the importance of properly researching window options and cost.

STOREY-HEIGHT WINDOWS

Incorporating a window which runs from the ground to underside of roof, maybe through both first and second floors, can be dramatic. You can often achieve this in a hallway or at a staircase position in a new home. The whole character of an existing house can be changed by introducing a storey-height window. They inject a wow factor into the hall or entrance of a home

BAY WINDOWS

These can be constructed in many formats (see Figure 6.2). I've used on many occasions a cantilevered bay - a window that sits out from the face of the external wall, supported on brackets back onto the wall. This allows you to construct a seat inside the room and also increases your vision out of the room. It's a great feature and is relatively cost-effective as it

doesn't involve building foundations. Alternatively, a proper bay can be formed, which does involve building foundations, but enables you to put furniture in the bay (see illustration 6.3).

LARGE SASHES

An impressive feature that appeared during the later Georgian periods was the same kind of vertical sliding sash window but used at a massive scale whereby the bottom sash lifts up and you can actually walk out from the reception room to the garden.

GLAZING

Glazing technology now offers many options. You can have energy-saving features such as low 'e' glass (low emissivity, which reduces heat losses) or triple glazing with gas filling the gaps between panes of glass. Where you have glass below 800mm above floor level it has to be toughened, which adds to the expense particularly if you're using double or triple glazing combined with low 'e' properties. You can fundamentally alter the way your home looks by selecting different window frames with sub-divisions and different glass. Take care if using double or triple glazing within small panes of glass, as this can look very heavy. Leaded lights can be faked quite easily by the careful

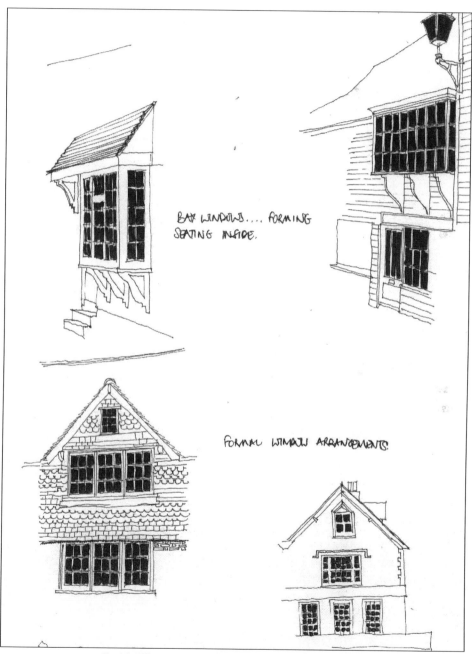

Fig 6.3 Different styles and configurations of window design

Fig 6.4 Examples of different bay windows

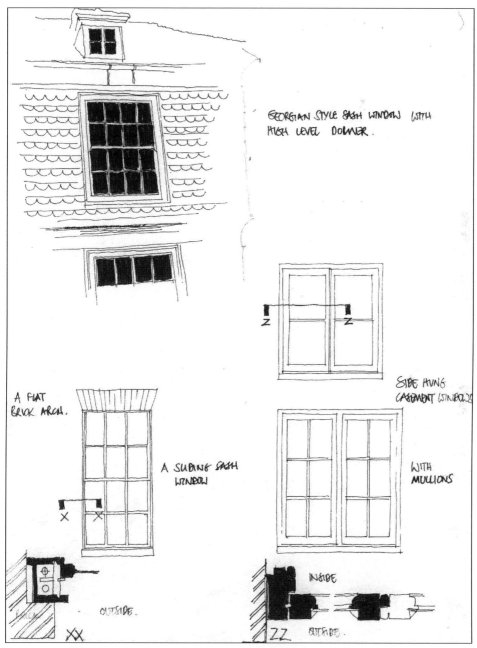

Fig 6.5 Examples of window types

application of lead tape either side of a window pane. If done carefully, this can look really convincing. Real leaded lights can still be made but are extremely expensive.

EXTERNAL DOORS

There are enormous choices for front or feature doors (see Figures 6.5 and 6.6). You can buy off-the-shelf oak, softwood, semi-glazed or metal (high security) doors. Some come pre-fitted into a frame, giving high standards of draught sealing. Research this feature carefully - if it's well designed, your front door will not only keep the draughts out but provide the right impression on entering your home. There might be other external doors from living spaces into gardens, so don't forget the option of using a sliding or folding door to open the whole room up to a spectacular view. Don't try and skimp on doors, buy the best as they get a lot of weather exposure and use. If possible, buy a door that you've seen in someone else's home, so that you understand how they work and can see that they have proved themselves through a track record of weather resistance and frequent use.

EXTRA-WIDTH DOORS

A wider than average door to the front of a house is a nice feature and helps

Fig 6.6 Front doors and porches

Fig 6.7 Front doors and porches

create an impressive entrance.

SECURITY

There should always be a security system. As well as good locks, you should be able to see whoever's outside before you open the door.

DOOR SILLS

These need to be considered carefully now in order to comply with the latest building regulations. The current aim is to enable a wheelchair-user, or less ambulant person, to come in and leave without tripping over a door sill.

STABLE DOORS

This type of door is a useful design features, ideal for a back door or the door from a utility room to the outside. They allow good ventilation but preserve some security. Stable doors with glazed top halves can look attractive.

ROOFS

Natural roof covering materials include terracotta or clay tiles, slate, stone or cedar shingles. Reconstituted or man-made materials include metal (lead, copper or zinc, for example), bituminous felts used in flat roofs and concrete fibre cement.

I've seen so many new homes, alterations or extensions where a poor

Fig 6.8 Stylish gable detailing

quality material has ruined the design effect. Spend time looking at the alternatives - it definitely pays off and you don't have to spend a fortune to achieve the right effect. Look around your area to find out what materials have been used locally. Go to the big roof finish manufacturers (listed on homedesign-online.co.uk) and ask for sample materials so you can see and handle what you're buying. Look at a roof that's been constructed in this material. Remember that your choice of material depends on the pitch or angle of your roof. There's enormous choice of reconstituted materials now that look convincingly like the real thing but at a lesser cost.

EAVES DETAILING

You have many choices here. For example, a cottage or a more rustic

Fig 6.9 Roofscapes

effect can be enhanced with exposed rafter feet. These are usually just cut and stained and gutters are supported on special brackets, as opposed to being fixed to a fascia or horizontal piece of timber at the eaves position.

MOULDINGS

Instead of fitting a plain horizontal and vertical pieces of timber at the eaves, think about using mouldings to enhance the quality and feel of the eaves finish (see fig 6.7).

GABLES

Gable ends usually have barge boards and there are some fabulous examples of decorative barge boards where joiners have had fun in incorporating detail and decorative features (usually the Victorian and Edwardian periods) (see fig 6.7).

RIDGES

This is the apex of the roof. With most roofing materials, you'll have to finish the ridge in a ridge tile. There's a range of decorative ridges, gargoyles and finials that could be appropriate to a particular home design.

VERGES

These are the edges of the roof. Different coloured mortars, used to bed in the end tiles, can have a large effect on the way a roof looks.

VALLEYS

With many tile materials it's possible to get special fittings to form the valleys where roof slopes meet. For some materials these aren't available and you only have the choice of using lead or a preformed glass fibre valley.

A method used in the past was lacing the tile right through the valley, termed as laced valleys. This avoids the use of a valley tile fitting and sweeps the tiling around through the two planes of roof.

PORCHES AND CANOPIES

A front door porch can be either a simple bracketed canopy over the door or a building constructed to form an outer covered area, or even a room, before entry. I've seen successful open porches where seats have been installed and can think of many examples of otherwise ugly houses uplifted and transformed by a really stylish porch.

Verandahs are elongated porches, usually running across the front or back of a building, allowing people to sit under cover and on a raised area. In this country it is very useful in that you can be outdoors when it is raining without getting wet! This is a particularly nice feature to include in chalet bungalows where glazing can be incorporated to allow light into internal rooms.

PORCH DESIGN

This can incorporate brackets, posts, piers, seats. Piers can be supported on metal shoes or even stone stools. Verandahs can include handrails and balustrading if there's a drop between a raised deck and the garden.

RAINWATER GOODS

Rainwater goods (gutters and downpipes) are available in cast iron, aluminium, lead or copper. They're also available in different sizes and cross-sections. They are a very important detail which doesn't have to add significantly to the overall cost of your home.

DESIGN FEATURES

■ Profiled gutter sections.
■ Decorative hoppers.
■ Decorative bracketing to support guttering and rainwater pipes.

COLOUR

Copper is effective as it produces a weathered green tint. Pre-coloured, maintenance-free finishes are also available, usually in aluminium. Colour co-ordinate rainwater goods with window and door colours.

CHIMNEYS, FLUES AND CHIMNEY POTS

Chimneys are usually constructed in brick and there's tremendous scope for introducing decorative brickwork, for example, indents, string courses, corbels and arches. All these features add interest. Chimneys are also available in stainless steel or coloured metalwork. There's an enormous range of chimney pots available in different colours and finishes but most are terracotta.

DESIGN FEATURES

■ Shaped and varying sections of chimney.
■ Decorative brickwork and special bricks.
■ Arched construction within chimneys.

ROOF WINDOWS

To resist exposure to weather, most roof windows are constructed in aluminium or metal. The position of the roof window relative to the roof plane is important. If you look at old properties you'll find that roof windows 'sit tight down' onto the roof plane.

PIVOTING OPTIONS

Choose either centre pivot or top-hung designs.
■ Escape windows. Roof windows can be used as fire escape windows

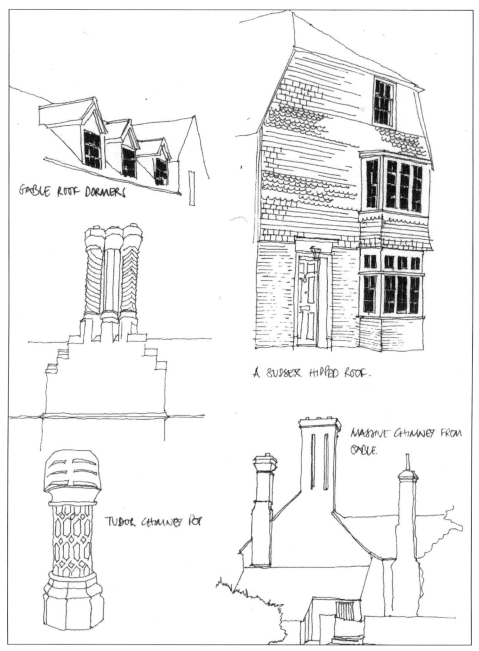

GABLE ROOF DORMERS

A SUSSEX HIPPED ROOF.

TUDOR CHIMNEY POT

MASSIVE CHIMNEY FROM GABLE.

Fig 6.10 Chimneys and roofscapes

provided they're hinged and positioned correctly relative to floor level. Some very sophisticated roof widows are available now where they open almost to form a dormer.

■ Advanced features. Roof windows can now incorporate rain sensors, black out blinds, venetian blinds, solar control glass and automatic operations from remote control.

EXTERNAL LIGHTING

This is covered in more detail in a Chapter 9. However, a wide range of fittings is available from the traditional style external lights, usually bracketed or bulkhead fittings, to the more modern style contemporary fittings, including concealed floor positioned built in fittings.

GARDEN DESIGN

Good garden design, including hard landscaping (drives, paths, patios) will enhance the value of the home. It also enhances your enjoyment and can even provide an outside 'room' during the summer, prolonged by outdoor heaters. Consider items such as a shed, jacuzzi, swimming pool and children's play equipment for inclusion in your brief so they can be integrated into the overall design. A properly designed garden can be low-maintenance.

INTERNAL HOME DESIGN DETAILS

STAIRCASES

Stairs are usually constructed in timber and many joinery manufacturers specialise in traditional handrail and balustrade, giving you plenty of choice. Stone staircases are also available at higher cost. If you're using stone, it's probably appropriate to use a metal balustrade or handrail. Metal staircases are often appropriate in contemporary homes - metal and glass balustrades and handrails can look spectacular. Staircases can take a number of forms:

■ spiral or semi-spiral

■ straight flight

■ dog leg flight

■ half landings

Winders in a staircase achieve a change of direction or preserve headroom or fit a stair into a confined space. There are also special space-saving stairs, which allow you to rise quickly within a confined space. Special staircase design features include decorative balustrades, special stair parts - bullnose steps, cantilevered treads, swept handrails and volutes where the handrail turns into a tight corner at the bottom of the staircase usually co-ordinated with a bullnose step. The string or side of the staircase can often be decorated or the treads may be on show as a design detail (common in Georgian buildings).

FIREPLACES

Fireplaces or fire surrounds are usually built in stone, brick or metal (usually cast iron). The choice is almost endless so look at the options provided by many manufacturers (see homedesign-online. co.uk). Timber fire pieces are also now popular (a typically Victorian detail). The types of fireplace available range from the traditional fire surround with hearth to wood burners, double sided fireplaces or wood burning stoves. There are also many variations on styles from Victorian, Georgian and Edwardian to contemporary styles.

FLOOR TILES

The main materials are terracotta, stone, ceramic and vinyl. One of my main concerns in selecting a floor tile is to make sure it fits in with the interior environment, which normally reflects the architectural style of the building. There's a huge variety of colour, texture, pattern and relief.

Ceramic tiles lend themselves to under-floor heating systems. Take care to check the manufacturer's requirements for under-floor heating beneath vinyl floor finishes.

WOODEN FLOORS

Types of floor include traditional planked, tongue and grooved wood and veneered manufactured floors. There's a good choice of wooden floor products and you need to take into account width, colour, material and finish. Some of the veneered manufactured floors can look very convincing and provide a surface that's much more resistant to damage and staining than natural timber.

MOULDINGS AND PANELLING

I'm referring here to any type of timber or plaster moulding, including skirtings, dado rails, covings, architraves, picture rails and panelling. The are scores of products available off-the-shelf. MDF (medium density fibreboard) has allowed many possibilities for these details ready for decoration. Panelling, which was widespread during the Victorian and Georgian periods, is being revived in modern home design and produces a wonderful decorative effect. It really needs to be installed carefully at either half the height of the room or full height in one or two rooms.

RADIATORS, SWITCHES AND POWER POINTS

With each of these I recommend going for good quality. Such functional items really matter. Switches especially get a lot of use and so high quality pays off.

INTERNAL DOORS

The various manufacturers provide lots of options including framed, ledged and braced cottage-style doors, plain painted doors, glazed doors, panelled doors, stable doors and sliding or folding door systems allowing you to open up or close off two rooms. Choose appropriately styled ironmongery and go for good quality because door furniture is used a great deal.

USE OF COLOUR

Paint manufacturers can match just about any colour you want and also give you good ideas on co-ordinating colours, including suggestions on finishes. It's a matter of personal taste but I feel that a matt or silk finish to joinery (internal doors, windows, skirtings and architraves) looks so better than gloss.

SPECIAL DESIGN FEATURES

Listed below are some home design features I've used in new homes and in alterations. This is just a brief list but it might prompt you to think about the sort of design features you could adopt in your project:

■ pre-formed niches help break up a wall or provide a feature at a corner position
■ external window shutters controlled electrically are a great security feature if you leave your home unattended for any length of time
■ internal window shutters which can be hinged wooden panels that fold back into the window reveal - a really neat idea, giving a feeling of snugness and security, and you can still have curtains
■ bay window seats on brackets provide a useful additional piece of furniture
■ lay out your rooms so that you can incorporate built-in cupboards

DESIGNING FOR CHILDREN

These are some feature to include to keep children safe:

■ stair gates and safe balustrades
■ protection to low window sills both at ground and, especially, first floor level
■ child locks on windows (at first floor check whether a window is an escape window)
■ adequate space in a family bathroom to allow access to children in baths and other areas
■ open planning for kitchen, living and dining areas to make child supervision a great deal easier – aim for good visibility from the kitchen to the garden, approach from the road and drive
■ power point protection

DESIGN FOR THE ELDERLY

To increase user-friendliness for elderly visitors, guests or, maybe, yourself incorporate:

■ no thresholds to trip over when entering your home (now a building regulation requirement).

■ adequate door widths to all rooms on the ground floor (now a building regulation requirement).

■ a good amount of space in front and around a WC

■ position light switches and power points for people who are less mobile (now a building regulation requirement).

■ strong lighting in 'work areas', such as in kitchen and bathrooms, so it's possible to see clearly what's going on

■ easy-to-use door furniture and light and power switches

■ low surface temperature radiators to prevent burning

DESIGN FOR SECURITY

Security is an increasing concern and the following design features can help make your home safe:

■ external lights on sensors

■ mains powered smoke detector with emergency battery backup – few householders check batteries regularly so mains operation is a good idea, with battery back-up on trickle charge when not in use

■ front door security chain locks and spy peepholes so you can check who's there before you open the door, adjust the

layout of your home to improve security, for example, windows overlooking the drive and entrance and fencing the garden to make it more difficult for someone to enter uninvited

■ fit security locks on windows and doors - this can reduce insurance premiums and some insurance companies actually require this

CHAPTER 7

DESIGN AND CONSTRUCTION METHODS

From a design perspective, what do you actually want when it comes to the construction of your new home, alteration or extension? Surveys have found that most home owners want robustness, permanence, sound insulation and a good sale value. My experience suggests people want all this and more. Home owners are interested in how their home looks and feels. Many want flexibility for change and everyone is interested in putting their stamp of individuality in their home. This might be through a particular design feature or the way their home has been constructed or altered. Figure 7.1 is a quick reference for design characteristics and construction types.

With recent advanced in construction technology you have a wonderful choice in terms of the construction system you select. In this chapter I describe the main types of construction method and list the advantages and disadvantages from a home design point of view.

BRICK AND BLOCK CONSTRUCTION

The most popular home construction method is still load-bearing masonry, that is, walls comprising blockwork on the inside supporting the structure, a cavity and then brickwork, or similar material, on the outside. This kind of traditional cavity wall construction has

# CHAPTER SEVEN ● DESIGN AND CONSTRUCTION METHODS

been used for well over 100 years but could be coming to an end - it's messy, time consuming to construct and it's becoming increasingly difficult to achieve the high standards of insulation now required by building regulations, especially in view of new standards likely to come into force.

Masonry construction might still have a future, if new technologies are incorporated, such as thin joint technology. This is one of a few new fast construction systems becoming more popular. It's been developed by a company called Celcon and uses a rapid-setting thin joint mortar with normal size blocks (440mm x 215mm) and a jumbo block (440mm x 330mm). Celcon claims a seven-day saving of labour on a typical house over conventional block-laying. Eventually, it should be possible to build a house and put the roof on before constructing the outside wall, or skin, of brick or other external material. This will be achieved through greater accuracy of the components. The smaller joints also achieve good air tightness and avoid cold spots through gaps or joints. Additionally, this method promotes much cleaner sites, speed of erection and, I believe, has a great future provided the labour force learns and adapts.

Also developed by Celcon is the Jämera house system, which involves the use of aircrete (the material blockwork is made from). Jämera is a building system established some time ago in Finland, using tongue and groove reinforced concrete elements enabling ground, upper floors and roof to be constructed of the same components. This sort of system has great potential as it prefabricates building components in factory conditions, minimises the time on site, provides good insulation and avoids cold spots through bridges of different materials. The system can also be used for roofs over traditional brick and block walls, which allows roof spaces to be open, either for use as a separate floor or as part of open roof to first floor rooms below. A similar system is produced by another manufacturer, Marshalls. Here wall panels comprise two skins of cement particle board with a rigid urethane core to create a composite panel.

ADVANTAGES
- durability and robustness
- longevity of life
- perceived as sound and reliable by house buyers
- solid feel and less noise transmission (50% greater sound insulation than plasterboard and stud partitions)
- flexibility for change
- solid floors can be supported between floor levels
- easy for DIY fixings

103

DISADVANTAGES
■ slower to build on site (new systems will reduce construction time)
■ struggles to meet building regulation insulation standards

Once the new technologies have become established, it's likely that the advantages timber frame currently enjoys over masonry construction will be overtaken. Brick and block construction has a future but it might be a few years before the new methods really take off

TRADITIONAL HOME VERSUS TIMBER FRAME

TIMBER FRAME
Timber frame is the most popular home construction method in the UK after masonry. The two countries of origin of timber frame are Canada and Scandinavia. Both have a considerable track record in developing and building frame houses. With this type of construction the inside load-bearing wall comprises timber frame, which is infilled with insulation material and generally achieves much higher standards than equivalent blockwork. Internal dividing walls are formed by plasterboard and timber stud partitions. Ground floors are usually concrete with the upper floors being timber construction. Timber frame is well established now in this country

and there are many suppliers who can just provide the timber frame kit or see the whole project through from start to completion. Some of these companies are listed on www.homedesign-online.co.uk. Other types of timber frame construction include post and beam. This consist of vertical posts and horizontal beams made up of timbers typically 100mm x 100mm (4in x 4in) in section to 200mm x 300mm (8in x 12in) in section up to lengths of 5 metres (16ft).

ADVANTAGES
■ timber is a beautiful material and can look fantastic viewed from both inside and outside
■ post and beam allows barn-like proportions lending itself to open planning, large storey heights and feature windows
■ allows contemporary and traditional designs, for instance medieval oak frames exposed inside and outside or contemporary style timber frames, again exposed internally and externally
■ quick erection of frame on site – typically one or two weeks
■ low embodied energy - softwood is a renewable material that doesn't involve a lot of energy in production
■ generally efficient to heat

DISADVANTAGES
■ needs a lot of pre-planning and factory

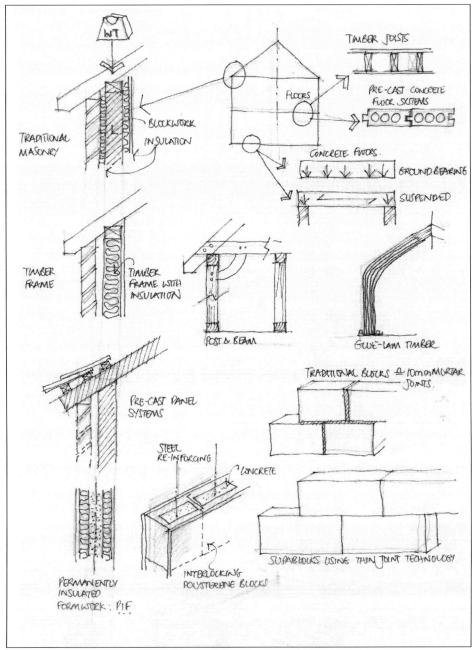

Fig 7.1 The different types of instruction

time before construction can start

■ not flexible to incorporate changes

■ difficult to incorporate insulation in post and beam type construction

■ trades people in this country are less familiar with timber frame than other construction methods

■ noise insulation is generally good inside to outside but not within the house

■ does not lend itself to basement or underground construction

■ suspicion among home buyers can affect re-sale value

■ fixing internal fittings - brackets, shelves, kitchen units and pictures – is not easy

For building a new home, timber is a lovely material to use. There's scope to use the material so it's visible inside and outside, leading on, perhaps, to timber decks and other timber features. You can achieve good air tightness with timber construction and create very energy efficient designs. If this interests you, look into the new Canadian super energy efficient homes (termed Super E) which are now being developed in the UK. It's reckoned that between a third and a half of all heat is lost by way of unintentional draughts - Super E homes have to pass an air pressure test. Canadian airtight houses provide indoor air quality by the use of a whole house ventilation system which we come back to in chapter 8.

There are advantages in using timber frame at a first-floor level in a two-storey extension to reduce weight and increase space by building a single studwork thickness clad on the inside and outside. As far as alterations are concerned, timber frame can be useful to reduce weight and make for easier and less messy construction than blockwork alternatives. Specialist advice is needed when altering an existing timber frame.

PERMANENTLY INSULATED FORMWORK (PIF)

As the name implies, this method involves the use of formwork or shuttering to form concrete walls. The formwork remains in place providing insulation and is clad in finishing materials inside and outside. This is another fast track system and is currently promoted in this country by a company called Becowallform. The Beco system is based on large hollow lightweight blocks which lock together (without intermediate bedding materials) to provide a formwork into which concrete is poured. Once set, the concrete becomes a high strength structure and the formwork remains in place as thermal insulation. Bearing in mind thermal insulation requirements are going to be tightened over the next five years, Beco claims that by 2010 its system will result in heat losses 30-45% lower than the standard. These sorts of system have a great future in terms of zero energy consumption, which is a concept of the future but not very far away.

PIF is a completely new construction system in this country but has a proven track record - it was developed over 25 years ago and has been used extensively in Europe. It also lends itself to underground construction including basements. PIF has advantages in terms of revolutionising finishing methods, not only to the outside but to the inside of homes, as finishes are fixed direct to the insulation formwork.

ADVANTAGES
■ creative designs using the comprehensive range of products available - curves, basements and storey-height windows
■ very high performance for fire resistance and acoustic insulation in relation to current and future building regulations
■ fast construction saving time and cost
■ well tried and tested in Europe
■ option to clad inside or outside in any material
■ solid permanent feel

DISADVANTAGES
■ some systems more suited to institutional type buildings involving repetition of openings and somewhat inflexible for bespoke designs
■ in Europe walls are often rendered with relatively little brick and timber cladding so the system is perhaps not so suited to UK vernacular
■ specialist, experienced labour force advisable for construction
■ relatively heavy on foundation loads

I am fascinated by this construction concept and, if I were building a new home, I would seriously consider its use. I think a basement is essential in new houses, where practical, and with PIF the same construction system can be used throughout.

UNDERGROUND HOMES AND BASEMENTS
There are two main methods of constructing underground homes and basements: first, in-situ (constructed on site) cast shuttered concrete (reinforced masonry or reinforced concrete) or, second, pre-cast (manufactured in factory conditions) concrete wall panels. Optimistic construction cost figures are quoted by the industry but don't be fooled – underground construction is expensive, especially as builders and specifiers are very wary of getting involved in a system that could leak. Despite the costs, basements do provide extra space

which is highly energy efficient and the 3-storey bungalow (a chalet bungalow with basement) can be a useful design concept.

I suggest always considering including a basement when you're building a new home or carrying out a large scale extension or alteration. Carry out a proper analysis with professional help to establish water levels and feasibility of construction. Go for the best possible system, which might include belt and braces solutions whereby you incorporate a waterproof construction system and a drainage system to relieve water pressure. Don't be tempted by the cheapest option. With an average increase of 50% more floor area to your existing home, you could add significantly to the value of your new home. Get advice at the feasibility stage on costs of construction relative to a re-sale value (see Chapter 2).

With underground homes, or earth-sheltered homes, the systems of construction are similar to that used with basements. The big difference is the roof, which is usually a pre-cast concrete system brought onto the site or steel reinforced concrete made on site. This is then waterproofed and insulated, before it's covered in grass or soil. Somewhere between 375mm and 450mm (15in and 18in) provides a typical roof build-up including structure, insulation and soil.

ADVANTAGES

■ providing accommodation below ground can be a persuasive argument with planning officers where they would otherwise resist development

■ extra space (otherwise unachievable) in a basement can significantly increase home value

■ energy savings - zero heat loss should be achievable

■ low maintenance - the construction is virtually unaffected by wind or weather

■ security

■ low fire risk

DISADVANTAGES

■ can be dark – lighting needs careful planning

■ skill and time are required in underground construction, which inevitably leads to higher cost

■ doesn't lend itself to DIY as it requires high standards of design, workmanship and supervision

■ potential for building defects

OTHER FRAME BUILDINGS

Steel frame Steel frame is similar to timber frame systems and is usually used where the home owner or architect wants to achieve a particular, most often modern, building effect. Materials such as stainless steel, zinc, glass lend themselves to this construction system. There are many contemporary award-winning designs using steel frame.

ADVANTAGES

■ possibility of exciting designs, minimalist in character, including curved roof forms and exposed frames

■ allows open plan space giving hi-tech feel

■ potential for large openings

■ construction time on site is minimised, provided proper pre-planning is carried out

DISADVANTAGES

■ highly skilled work force required

■ long lead-in times to properly plan and work out detailing

■ skilled designer required to ensure proper detailing

■ structures require fire proofing - steel isn't as good as timber in fire

■ potential for cold bridging

■ protection and maintenance are issues.

STEEL FRAME

Steel frame lends itself to contemporary design styles for new homes. As far as extensions and alterations are concerned, a change in a structural system to steel can enable large window and door openings and also opening up roof spaces. A useful material.

GLUE LAM

Glue Lam timber is a series of thin sections of timber laminated with a specialist glue to provide large, long span beams. Through the process of lamination, shaped beams are achievable. It looks beautiful although is relatively expensive. There are usually no problems with cold bridging.

CONCRETE FRAMES

Reinforced concrete (concrete poured over steel reinforcing bars) can be employed instead of load-bearing steel, stud work or masonry. Form work is used to create the shapes required and, provided there's adequate reinforcement, the frame will work structurally. Again, it's used usually because the home owners, or their architect, wish to achieve a particular aesthetic quality.

ADVANTAGES

n great scope for forming mouldings with highly sophisticated form work

n wonderful textures and shapes can be achieved

n good fire rating

DISADVANTAGES

■ very costly

■ requires high level of expertise in the design process and construction

■ potentially for poor insulation and cold bridging leading to condensation

■ limited life and, if not properly detailed,

■ will cause staining to outside finished surfaces

OTHER DOMESTIC CONSTRUCTION SYSTEMS

Straw bales Bales are laid on edge and anchored with steel pegs to form walls. The outer surfaces are normally covered in a mesh and rendered inside and out. Because of settlement, straw bales are not usually used for supporting roofs and so a separate structural system is necessary, usually on the inside of the straw bale wall.

ADVANTAGES

■ very high standards of insulation - zero heat loss

■ sustainable material - nil O2 depletion.

■ Often enables use of a locally produced material

■ lends itself to use as part of an environmentally-friendly structure

DISADVANTAGES

■ vermin infestation is an issue if walls are not rendered properly

■ can't usually be load-bearing

■ roofs need to be supported independently

■ high level of maintenance

■ requires big overhang roof for protection

■ often unexpectedly complicated and expensive structure

SPRAYED CONCRETE

Reinforcing mesh, usually in sheets, forms whatever shape is required. A fine mesh is suspended inside the reinforcing mesh and then sprayed using a specialist concrete. Insulation is added to the outside of this concrete shell with a further sprayed finish to form a weathered-looking surface. This is an ideal system if you want to create a really unusual home à la Hobbit house, Teletubbies, or Flintstones.

ADVANTAGES

■ creates unique homes

■ opportunities for self-expression

■ organic forms are achievable

DISADVANTAGES

■ very expensive

■ difficult to prove compliance with building regulations

■ needs specialist design and contractor

■ inflexible to future changes

MODULAR CONSTRUCTION SYSTEMS

The modular construction concept is to pre-fabricate easily assembled sections or pods which are plugged together on site, minimising construction time. As much work as possible is done in factory conditions and pods are usually completely finished including tiles, sanitaryware, fitted wardrobes, carpet and even sometimes furniture. Modular housing has been developed and adopted in Scandinavia and is now being used and promoted in this country. Modular housing is being taken up by developers for multiple housing units and sustainable modular housing is being pioneered by the Peabody Trust in London.

ADVANTAGES

■ ideal solution for a difficult or inaccessible locations saving time on awkward sites or exposed locations

■ speed of construction on site

■ sustainable and low energy features can be incorporated

DISADVANTAGES

■ demands complete accuracy

■ not fully understood by most of the construction industry so needs specialist design and construction

■ restricts individuality in home design

OTHER WALL CONSTRUCTION SYSTEMS

These walling systems, such as rammed chalk and cob walls depend on location within the country, provide a nice vernacular style on which to develop your home design, alteration or extension. In the south east there's a form of construction called 'bungarush', which consists of flint or brick outer walls rammed with chalk

and lime inside. In the West County, cob walls are built with temporary shuttering set up either side and rock, stone, lime and smaller particles are all rammed down between the shutters.

ADVANTAGES

■ sustainable construction relying on local materials and a low level of skill

■ can look superb

■ reflects local traditions and character

DISADVANTAGES

■ relies on thickness for weather-resistance, which can be a problem if space is at a premium

■ care has to be taken to avoid frost getting into the structure and causing damage

GRID SHELLS

This is an example of using timber (often a local resource) in a very imaginative way. Curved roof forms can be achieved using the grid shell concept without cluttering inside spaces with support structure. The shell usually formed with a lattice for lathes fixed together to form a rigid shell. It's possible to create wonderful internal spaces; however, great levels of skill, knowledge and expertise in design and construction are required. These systems have a great future.

	SELECT ANY ONE OR A NUMBER OF CRITERIA	LIKELY CONST TYPE
	Fig 7.2 INITIAL IDEAS FOR SELECTING A CONSTRUCTION TYPE : NEW HOME OR AN EXTENSION TO AN EXISTING HOME	
1	AIR TIGHTNESS - Keen to use a whole house ventilation system	B C E
2	LOW ENERGY USE C	C
3	FLEXIBILITY IN DESIGN ON SITE / SCOPE FOR CHANGES	A
4	WANT A BASEMENT?	D
5	OPEN SPAN SPACES OPEN TO ROOF	
		F B
6	SPEED OF ERECTION ON SITE	B
7	HIGH ELEMENT OF DIY	A
8	FUTURE SALEABILITY B36 (Known system)	A
9	LOW HEIGHT BUILDING (PLANNING RESTRICTION)	G
10	INVISIBLE HOME!	D
11	DIFFICULT ACCESS SIT	B
12	MINIMAL STRUCTURE VISIBLE D	D F
13	LOW RUNNINGS / LOW MAINTENANCE	C F
HOW TO USE	**1** Select criteria, e.g. 4, 5, 6 & 7 **2** From criteria select the possible construction systems e.g. D, C, F, B	

THE CONSTRUCTION SYSTEMS	DETAIL - see
A Traditional masonry construction (as promoted	Brick / block / cavity
by The Traditional House Building Bureau)	Solid floor (fast floor systems)
	Traditional cut & pitch roofs
	Trussed rafters
B 'Fast track'	Thin joint blockwork systems (Celcon UK)
	Pre-fabricated masonry construction : Celcon Jamera
	Marshalls Panabloc
	Timber frame - Scanadian / Canadian origin
	Permanently insulated formwork, e.g. Becowallform
C Energy efficient	Timber frame - Scanadian / Canadian origin
	PIF (permanently insulated formwork Becowallform)
	Jamera & Panabloc as above
D Underground homes (or earth sheltered homes)	Permanently insulated formwork Becowallform
	Pre-cast panel systems
	In-situ concrete systems
Basements	Similar systems as above
E Achieving air tight construction	Super E timber frame
	Use of thin joint blockwork & equivalent systems
F Frame	Timber : Conventional Timber Frame Post & Beam
	Traditional oak frame
	Concrete frame
	Steel frame
F Finishes (special)	Brick
	Stone
	Renders
G Green buildings	Rainwater harvesting
	Sewage treatment, reed beds etc.
	Solar panels
H Extensions	Traditional masonry construction
	Modular extensions
	Timber frame packages for extensions

3 Consider options, e.g. D C *4* Prioritise! *5* Select option D - look at options via homedesign-online.co.uk.

CHAPTER 8
DESIGN AND ENERGY SAVING

There's much in the media about global warming and how it's getting wetter and hotter and more disasters are happening. But, how does this affect the design of your home? The greenhouse effect is caused by noxious gases, such as carbon dioxide, being released in the atmosphere. The more energy we consume, the more emissions we produce. For example, gases like CFCs contain chlorine, which destroy the earth's protective ozone layer, allowing through more rays from the sun. Pollution in the atmosphere stops the heat getting back out and the earth gets hotter. As a result of this trend, building regulations have been tightened to reduce energy consumption. Buildings account for almost half the energy used in the UK. Of this energy, 20% is used in the construction of the building and 80% in the lifetime of the building. You can make a significant difference to your energy consumption by taking measures in the way you build and manage your home. There are benefits – you'll enjoy a higher and healthier level of comfort at a lower cost. Remember also that when you build extensions, or carry out alterations, building regulations impose far more restrictions than in the past to control what you do (see Chapter 11).

HOW TO SAVE ENERGY

Here are a few suggestions to make your new home or extension more energy-efficient.

■ Siting

Consider the effect of the sun (referred to as passive solar energy). On the ground floor, incorporate south-facing windows, tall enough to allow the winter sun to penetrate deeply into your home. Remember to have large windows to the south and smaller ones to the north.

■ use timber as your prime building material

Without doubt, timber is the greenest structural material (with the lowest embodied energy). From a design perspective, it's a natural product, looks beautiful, can be worked easily and reduces the greenhouse effect on the planet. For example, UK-grown timbers, such as Douglas fir, look great when used as exposed timbers or for windows. I've used larch for weather-boarding, and home-grown cedar shingles must be one of the most ecological roofing and cladding materials around.

■ spend your money efficiently

The traditional approach is to cover a timber frame with bricks as an additional skin. However, I always consider a design in terms of efficiency within the building budget. There are other solutions, using lower embodied energy materials, which are quicker to build and provide weather-proofing with extra insulation for the same cost (e.g. timber cladding and render).

■ efficient layout

In working up your design, think about having fewer doors, more open-plan spaces, keeping plumbing together and wall storage on the north, east and west walls to help reduce heat loss (and increase insulation). Look into warm roof systems whereby the roof plane is the insulating layer, which allows roof voids to be kept warm and used as habitable space; it also avoids the need to ventilate and reduces draughts and, therefore, energy losses.

■ build tight, ventilate right

The concept here is to build air-tight, sealing the building to reduce losses through draughts and air movement through external building fabric. This is the Super 'E' concept and relies on an effective controllable ventilation system, in addition to having windows that open. Ventilation helps provide a comfortable and healthy environment by diluting or removing pollutants from within the house (moisture, volatile organic compounds, house dust mites, oxides of nitrogen, carbon dioxide and tobacco smoke). The most effective way to ventilate is to remove moisture (the greatest pollutant) at its source, in bathrooms and kitchens.

■ construct your home of insulation

At present, cellulose (recycled paper insulation) gives the best performance with the least cost to the environment. In the near future there'll be a wide range of such insulants (other natural materials could be straw, hemp and wool) being marketed with the advantage of being locally produced and not having to be imported. Plan ahead and build for the future by incorporating really high levels of insulation.

■ minimise potential for thermal bridges
These are weak spots in the external fabric where heat can track out, causing a thermal bridge. Care needs to be taken in your design to ensure insulation is continuous, because by increasing the level of insulation you increase the risks of cold spots where condensation could occur.

■ store energy in water
Water is highly efficient, inexpensive and versatile since you can easily move it around by pumping. So, for example, use radiators or better still under floor heating.

■ introduce buffer zones
A porch acts as an airlock, reducing ventilation heat-loss and providing extra insulation. A single-glazed conservatory on a west wall is helpful for drying clothes and can harvest solar energy in the late afternoon, helping to delay cooling at night.

■ consider the shape, size and layout and your design
These factors have a significant effect on thermal performance and building cost. For example, a simple square box offers most internal space for least external surfaces. A long, thin design, having a longer south face, gives much more scope for passive solar energy. A complicated plan and roof form (with dormers, for instance) will use a lot more energy in the construction stage. The message is 'keep it simple if you are looking to save energy'. Don't forget my crusade for basements!

■ include an efficient heating system
Reducing heating demand is an essential part of sustainable houses. At the moment, a gas-fired central system is probably the most effective and efficient currently available. As homes become better insulated the provision of hot water is becoming more important than space-heating. For example, a super 'E' home might need only one or two kilowatts of heat during cold winter periods, much of which can be provided by cooking, electrical equipment and body heat. I prefer condensing boilers as they are far more energy efficient, provided they are linked to well-designed heating systems that ensure the boiler works most of the time in their most efficient condensing mode. Underfloor heating is very efficient. n If you have radiators, fit thermostatic

radiator valves (TRVs) and a really good control system. An energy-efficient heating system is all about hi-tech controls and we'll cover this in more detail in Chapter 9.

■ modify your standard WC cisterns

This reduces water wastage drastically. Dual flush loos are excellent - depress the handle for a quick flush (just half the water in the cistern is used) or hold the handle down for a longer flush (the whole cistern of water is used). If you're really serious about being green, maybe you'll want to install a properly engineered composting toilet that uses no water for flushing and produces rich compost!

■ reduce electricity consumption

Do this in the design and selection of the electrical system and appliances to minimise the use and wastage of energy. For example, pay particular attention to freezers and refrigerators and monitor how they're working. Thermostats have a habit of failing, often causing units to run day and night. Include light pipes (highly reflective tubes connected to clear plastic hemispheres on the roof, which convey daylight into the building) to flood natural light into your interiors and reduce the need for electric lights in the daytime. Low-energy lighting is worth considering.

■ reduce your household water consumption

This can be achieved by relatively simple measures, such as reducing water use (and waste of hot and cold water) by installing spray taps, self-closing taps and electronic sensor taps. It's now feasible to collect rainwater then filter and store it for household use and to recycle it as 'grey water'. Weigh up the cost of these systems against the savings in water consumption as well as the positive contribution to the environment. Collect rainwater for your garden - it's much better for plants than tap water.

■ incorporate efficient windows

From a design perspective, the most efficient windows are large plain units without glazing bars, since they've less edge area (the edge is where most heat transfer takes place). Bear in mind that each layer of glass reduces solar gain as do net curtains. Fit thermal blinds to all windows and use them when daylight fails or rooms are not in use. Insulated curtains or shutters are an alternative but I favour the blinds as a cheap and simple solution.

■ Choose your site with care and be flexible

When designing your home - as I've said in Chapters 2, 3 and 4 - take into account your future needs. Don't fill your attic with roof trusses or you, or future owners, will forever curse this unusable space and might be forced to extend.

■ assess key aspects of a site

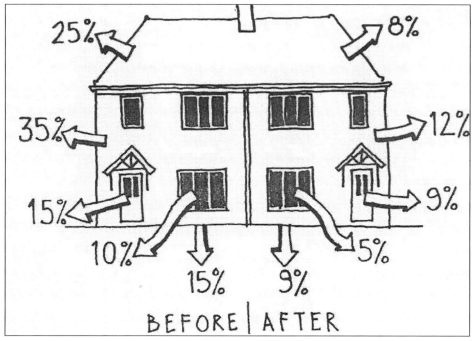

Fig 8.1 Benefits of insulating your home

Such as the local climate, potential for renewable energy (solar or wind), closeness to the infrastructure and support you need and attempt to predict any future changes which the surrounding locality might experience. This comes back to the importance of analysing your site and requirements properly. A house on a north-facing slope, with trees to the south, near a flood plain, or under power lines, will probably never be a good investment.

MAKING AN EXISTING HOME MORE ENERGY EFFICIENT

■ Construct a draught lobby or porch

This can make a big difference by providing an airlock to prevent heat losses.

■ Fit draught-proofing to doors and windows

A simple tip is to go round on a windy day with a candle or joss stick to see where wind is whistling through. You'll be surprised at where there are draughts, for example, around windows and doors, through power points, at the junctions of skirting boards and floors, through gaps in the floorboards, between ceilings and walls and around loft hatches. Air leakage also occurs around services – plumbing, gas and electrical - and through porous

FIG 8.2 TEN TIPS ON HOW TO SAVE ON YOUR HOME FUEL BILLS (IN COST ORDER)

	Cost	Annual Saving	Annual CO_2 saving (Kgs)
Only use the heat light & appliances you need	£0	between £15 - £40	190 - 500 kg
Lag your hot water tank	£5 - £10	between £10 - £15	125 - 190 kgs
Lag your hot water pipes	£5 - £10	between £5 - £10	60 - 125 kgs
Use energy saving lightbulbs	£5 - £15	£10	85 kgs
Add to your heating system - thermostat	£10 - £15	between £10 - £20	125 - 250 kgs
Add to your heating system - thermostatic radiator valves	£45 - £75	between £10 - £20	125 - 250 kgs
Add to your heating system - timer / programmer	£35 - £45	between £20 - £25	250 - 320 kgs
Fit Draughtproofing to windows and doors	£45 - £60	between £10 - £20	125 - 250 kgs
Loft insulation should be 200mm thick - DIY	£110 - £160	between £60 - £70	750 - 880 kgs
Loft insulation should be 200mm thick - Contractor	£190 - £300	between £60 - £70	750 - 880 kgs
Install plastic secondary double glazing	£120 - £600	between £15 - £25	190 - 320 kgs
If you have cavity walls, seek advice on cavity insulation	£300 - £500	between £60 - £70	750 - 880 kgs
If you have an old central heating boiler, fit an energy efficient condensing boiler	£400 - £600	between £100 - £130	1250 - 1700 kgs

materials. Seal such gaps to reduce air leakage.

■ Install low-energy light bulbs
Building regulations actually now require this in alteration works.

■ Move your fridge-freezer away from the oven to help improve efficiency.

■ Fit thermostatic radiator valves to your existing radiators
The thermostat on each radiator responds to particular conditions, which vary considerably over the floor plan of a house. A thermostatic radiator valve shuts the radiator down, conserving heat where it isn't required. They're relatively inexpensive and easy to fit.

■ Consider a high-efficiency self-condensing boiler.

■ Recycle both rainwater and grey water (see above).

■ Go open plan
When altering an interior, think about an open plan layout and altering existing window openings, to increase winter sun penetration (thereby reducing the need for electric light during the day). I've mentioned the idea of light tubes and can't over-emphasise the importance, when carrying out an alteration to your home, of increasing natural light.

■ Insulation, insulation, insulation
Wherever possible increase insulation in your roof space as this is where the majority of your heat is lost. Standards have increased from 50mm to 100mm, to now somewhere in the region of 300mm. Remember that when you increase

insulation in your home you must also allow adequate ventilation.

■ Consider central vacuum and simple heat recovery systems. These can often be integrated into an alteration or a refurbishment.

CONSTRUCTION AND ENERGY EFFICIENCY

I've mentioned that 20% of energy gets used up during construction. When you construct a building you'll have a choice of materials. Each material has an embodied energy figure, indicating the amount of energy used in the production of that material. These figures are a good indication of the amount of pollution created in its manufacture. Natural materials like wood are generally lower in embodied energy as it takes less energy to process them than, say, steel or plastic. Careful choice of materials during the design process helps reduce the embodied energy in your home and so reduce the effect its construction has on the environment.

Look at the construction process sequence to try to reduce on-site labour. Where possible, order locally produced materials to reduce transport costs and associated energy use. Avoid excessive trips to the builders' merchants, for example, if you're hiring a digger for digging foundations, double this up with

other excavation work. Minimise waste materials and ask your builder about recycling construction waste. Skips are expensive so you'll be saving your money if you reduce the wastage on site. Reduce cut-off waste and re-use what you do have – maybe use wood off-cuts for shelves or spare bricks in landscaping the garden. Use salvaged materials where you can, for example, second-hand tiles and bricks. There are a growing number of reclamation yards and prices can be lower than the equivalent new products. Make sure salvaged materials are safe, however, and don't compromise energy efficiency or water efficiency by installing old systems. Avoid highly processed materials where you can - use natural floor finishes like Sea Grass or Linoleum and non-toxic paints. Be aware of the noxious gases given off by some new materials, for example, formaldehyde in plywood and chipboard. For a healthier environment include plenty of plants.

RENEWABLE ENERGY

I have already talked through the principles of building a well insulated, airtight building to minimise heat losses, and these are to always be considered the first step measures in providing a very energy efficient home. Another environmentally-friendly aspect to the design to help the environment (and hopefully save money too) is the incorporation of renewable energy (RE) technologies (sometimes referred to as Low or Zero Carbon technologies). This term includes solar, wind, hydropower (from water), and the burning of natural waste products (wood pellets, logs and straw). Non-renewable energy comes from oil, coal, and gas - fossil fuels that will run out one day. The process of turning fossil fuels into energy, to heat water or provide electricity, produces the greenhouse gases which harm the atmosphere so any utilisation of RE can reduce impact on the environment. In fact, you're already using RE in your home, passively as heat gain through the windows from the sun. A by-no-means exhaustive list of the RE technologies available is as follows:

SOLAR HOT WATER PANELS

These are devices that collect the energy of the sun and deliver it as useful heat. The heat is captured in a collector, usually using pumped water, and stored in a hot water cylinder. These panels can be fitted to any type of heating system boiler, and supply a hot water cylinder with two coils. One coil will provide heating from the solar panel, and the second coil provides back-up from the system boiler when necessary.

These panels are at their most efficient when fitted to roof slopes with a southerly orientation, the most efficient being at an angle of between 40 and 45 degrees on a south-facing roof.

SOLAR PHOTOVOLTAIC (PV) CELLS

Not to be confused with solar hot water panels, PV cells convert sunlight into electricity. They are clean, quiet, maintenance free and efficient in their use of solar energy.

PV is the most expensive renewable energy option, with current prices varying between £4,000 and £6,000 per kW installed. For a standard house that would equate to around £28,000 of PV cells in order to generate the amount of power needed. Buying that electricity from the grid would cost around £600 per year, giving a payback period of 46 years. However, the system would save little over two tonnes of CO_2 per year.

Other than in a remote rural location, the panels will always need to be connected to the National Grid to sell on excess electricity. You should check with your provider for information on this.

WOOD BURNING STOVES

In certain circumstances with a well insulated and designed house a wood burning stove can supply all the heat required.

Wood burning stoves also provide an extremely attractive focus for a room. In

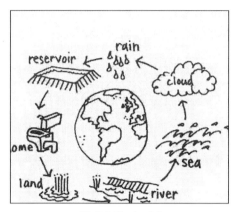

Fig 8.2 The 'cycle'

our experience, the use of wood burning stoves is also viewed favourably by the local planning department.

BIOMASS BOILERS

Biomass simply refers to the use of non-fossil fuels (such as wood in the form of logs, chips or pellets), to power a specialised boiler. The fuel is virtually carbon-neutral - the CO_2 produced as a result of combustion is taken as being no more than the CO_2 absorbed while it was growing.

There are still issues with the supply of fuel, as it is bulky and the costs of transport are high. Biomass boilers are generally aimed at rural houses, which have access to local reliable source of local timber and have sufficient storage space. The availability of biomass fuels is still not that good, but it is improving all the time.

In our experience, the use of biomass

is always viewed favourably by the local planning department. However, if it is specified within a planning application, they may apply a condition to ensure it is included as part of the project.

HEAT PUMPS

There are two main types of heat pump – those that take latent heat from the ground (Ground Source), and those that take latent heat from the air (Air Source). A heat pump is simply a refrigerator in reverse. Heat Pumps are not wholly renewable energy because they do use electricity to run (though the electricity could be generated from a renewable source). They are however an efficient way of using non-renewable energy to heat the home.

GSHPs have a Coefficient of Performance (CoP) of between 300% - 500%, which means that for every 1kW of electricity you put in, you will get 3, 4 or 5kWs of heat out. This makes them up to five times more efficient than the most efficient mains gas fired boilers. ASHP systems are essentially air conditioning units that run in reverse. They have a low CoP of around 1.5 in the winter, and tend to only have a small output. ASHPs heat pumps advertise a higher CoP of around 3, with outputs between 3kW and 17kW, but have a lower capital cost than that of GSHPs.

Although not as much electricity is required per unit of heat output (due to the benefit of the CoP) mains electricity is more expensive currently than the gas for a gas boiler alternative. GSHPs are more efficient than ASHPs but also more expensive and a good area of land (or a bore hole) is required for the pipe run.

GSHPs are generally robust, reliable technology. A properly designed system needs no back-up system and will, with correct servicing, last 15 to 20 years. Whilst they cost more than a comparable gas- or oil-fired boiler, they are gradually falling in price.

GOVERNMENT INCENTIVES

There are financial incentives available from the Government for these types of technologies. Feed-in Tariffs (FITs) were introduced in the UK in April 2010, and in essence pay the homeowner a set amount for every unit of electricity that is generated. This incentive will help reduce the length of the payback period. Renewable Heat Incentives (RHIs) are due for introduction in April 2011. This will apply to renewable energy technologies that produce heat rather than electricity, such as heat pumps and biomass boilers. The RHI is paid to the homeowner for every kilowatt-hour (kWh) of heat energy produced. The exact amounts to be paid have yet to be agreed, but will be dependent on the size of the system. As with FITs, these payments will help reduce the payback period for the initial capital outlay, and offset the costs of the fuel used, thus saving money.

design 1 · analysis 2 · site 3 · design 4 · styles 5 · details 6 · construction 7 · energy saving 8 · services 9 · costs 10 · regulations 11

CHAPTER 9

PLUMBING, ELECTRICAL AND DRAINAGE SYSTEMS

HEATING AND PLUMBING

We've all been in houses where rooms have been too hot, too cold, too stuffy or too draughty. At some stage, we've probably been woken up in the morning by creaking and banging central heating pipes and clattering cold water service pipes (caused by water hammer). Careful design and a professional installation enable you to avoid these problems. You've the opportunity to get it right whether you are building a new home, an extension or carrying out an alteration. This is what I suggest you do.

Prepare a written performance specification with your home designer, prior to seeking a fully detailed specification and drawings from the plumbing designer who's actually providing a price. Specify the type of sanitary ware and your requirements for heating and hot water. For instance, whether you want to be able to have two showers running at the same time or want to split the upstairs and downstairs into heating zones. This all means more work at the drawing board stage but it's worthwhile as it'll ensure all systems installed will be compatible and operate satisfactorily. Think about appointing a consultant to design the scheme or employ a suitably qualified design-and-build plumbing contractor. Either should have professional indemnity insurance to cover design problems. Architects or other professional advisers ought to be able to recommend appropriate a local plumbing designer. Architects don't usually have the necessary expertise themselves to write a detailed specification for plumbing services.

Any contractor working on gas installations must be a 'Corgi' registered installer and it's desirable that your plumber should also be a member of The Institute of Plumbing (IOP). The Heating and Ventilation Contractor's Association (HCVA) can suggest suitably qualified installers. Only employ your builder's favourite plumber or the plumber who quotes the cheapest price, if you're totally confident about that selection. Take advice from your installer ensuring the equipment is selected for long life, proven reliability, ease of maintenance and availability of spares. A proficient installer will fit the equipment so that access is available for regular maintenance and not hidden behind walls, panels or other equipment. Minor problems soon become major ones if joints leak or equipment fails and the plumber or engineer can't get to the cause of the problem.

Government is increasingly taxing fuels in an attempt to reduce consumption and, therefore, reduce ozone depletion gasses. Investigate fuel options and the various incentive schemes for using energy-efficient boilers. Always have in mind wall and roof insulation, double glazing and draught proofing.

SYSTEMS AVAILABLE

Here is a summary of the current range of heating and plumbing products for you to consider.

SANITARY WARE:

When selecting sanitary ware (wash-hand basins, toilets, baths, taps and showers) check whether they require a large volume of water, as this is dependent on:
■ cold water main size
■ cold water tank size
■ hot water tank size
■ water pressure
■ boiler size
■ running cost (if your water is metered)

Pipes must be sized correctly to ensure there'll be no noise or water hammer and that there'll be good flow and pressure. With careful thought and design, you can disguise pipe work or position it out of direct view. With an extension or alteration you'll probably be adding onto an existing system. Take advice on the suitability of this system to handle the changes or cope with additional sanitary ware required. Hot water storage: Where once the insulated copper cylinder was the only way of storing hot water, there's now a choice of unvented hot water, small quick-recovery cylinders and thermal stores. Water in a traditional cylinder usually flows from the cold water storage tank in the loft and flow rate is limited to this pressure, so showers generally need to be pumped. The cylinder needs to be below the level of the cold water tank and so often occupies valuable storage space. It takes 20 to 30 minutes to heat up a full tank of water. Alternatively, there are now quick-recovery cylinders, which allow it to be smaller and, consequently, easier to accommodate. These cylinders can be vented or unvented (see below). There are also mains pressure cylinders, fed directly at mains water pressure rather than via a cold water tank in the loft. This system produces better flow rates and often eliminates the need for pumped showers.

HEATING FUELS:

■ Gas from the main is clean and cheap and generally readily available in built-up areas, where a gas main runs within 25 metres of your home. If you haven't got mains gas, liquid petroleum gas (LPG) might be appropriate, if you want to cook with gas. It costs more than mains gas and you need storage tanks or bottles, which can be an eyesore.

■ Heating oil is the next best solution, if gas isn't available and is now available at competitive prices. You have to have a storage tank (a full tank should last for some months). Oil heating can smell in certain locations especially if the placement of the boiler and flue are not considered properly.

■ Electricity is relatively expensive but electric under-floor heating for small areas can be appropriate (for instance, bathrooms and kitchens).

■ Solid fuel, such as timber, Coalite or Phurnacite, are an alternative which might be appropriate in more isolated locations. They require special boilers or burners, storage space, manhandling and stoking.

BOILERS:

■ High efficiency condensing boilers are now a must under the new building regulations when fitting new boilers.

■ Combination (combi) boilers heat water on demand thus avoid the need for storage.

■ Vented or unvented systems: In the UK, the traditional heating pipe circuit is open to the air at some point or vented, which means that it has a header tank for expansion and topping up (usually located in the attic). The modern alternative is a sealed, unvented system. This operates under pressure (usually 1.5 bar) and carries hot water more efficiently than

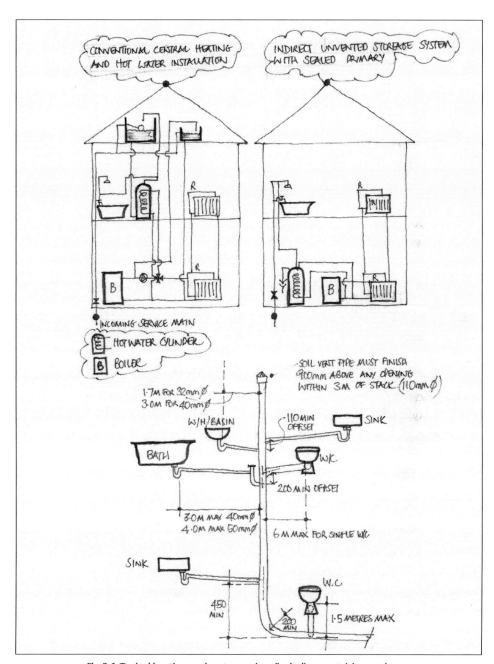

Fig 9.1 Typical heating and water services (including waste) in your home

a vented system. This system is filled directly from the water mains and so doesn't require a header tank, thus freeing up attic space. It's also less prone to frost damage and contamination via the open header tank.

FLUES:

■ A balanced flue is the simplest of the current flue options available. The boiler must sit on an outside wall because the flue exits via the back of the boiler through the wall, extending up to 400mm from the back of the boiler.

■ Fanned flues rely on a heat-resistant fan to pull the burnt fuel through into the fresh air. They can be run up to three or four metres from the boiler position which allows more flexibility in the placement of the boiler.

■ The vertex flue combines the principle of the vertical open flue with the balanced flue. It can rise from the boiler and exit through a flat or pitched roof. Flues measure around 150mm in diameter and can run up to four or five metres.

RADIATORS:

Radiators are available in a range of shapes and sizes, colours, patterns and finishes to suit all applications

■ conventional radiators - panel radiators

■ low surface temperature radiators - ideal for rooms used by the very young or

very old

■ column radiators - bulbous, cast iron sections bolted together which give high outputs with a traditional feel

■ skirting radiators - run within the skirting board profile at floor level

■ fanned convectors - typically an overhead version for bathrooms or a kick-board design that fits into the space under kitchen units and can include time clocks enabling them to be turned on and off automatically

■ trench radiators - run in a channel in the floor covered by a grille, and under-floor heating

■ Under-floor heating: Wherever you can, consider using under-floor heating. This isn't just for new homes - it can be included in extensions or alterations. Under-floor heating is available as a wet system, with pipe work either under or within a floor carrying hot water, or as an electric alternative, ideal for bathrooms. Under-tile warmers are cost-effective and easy to install. You might still need back-up heating via a radiator. In my experience, home-owners adapt to and come to appreciate under-floor heating. It spreads heat evenly and is particularly suitable for rooms with large ceiling heights, such as barn conversions. It's also energy-efficient and allows the temperature in each room to be individually controlled.

FIG 9.2 HELP IN CHOOSING A RADIATOR	
SELECT FROM THE FOLLOWING CRITERIA	RADIATOR TYPE SEE WWW.HOMEDESIGN-ONLINE.CO.UK. (CHAPTER 10) FOR MANUFACTURERS DETAILS
Contemporary home : stylish, sculptural radiators 'on display'	Column, low level finned, coloured, sculptural shapes, wall panels hung as pictures etc.
Invisible : no radiators	Underfloor heating, trench radiators
Period property : need to select an early style radiator	Column or segmental radiators
Requirement for underfloor heating just in kitchens and bathrooms (assuming a tiled floor)	Electric under tile warmers
Lose radiator 'in the wall'	Plain panel radiators with flat surface painted out the same colour as the wall
Low level around the room	Skirting radiators
Having fun in the bathroom! Use of sculptural radiators as towel rails	Spirals, corkscrew, adder, wavey : chrome / or different colours

HEATING CONTROLS:

Good heating and hot water controls enable greater energy efficiency and more comfortable conditions. They can include complex weather compensating systems, especially with under-floor heating, and features such as optimisation which seek to maximise boiler efficiency by predicting demand by analysing past performance. The heating and hot water systems must be controlled by a central source control, which varies water temperature automatically whatever the external conditions to maintain a cylinder temperature of 60°C.

You can control the temperature of individual rooms by using thermostatic radiator valves (TRVs), thus rooms not in constant use can be left cool or just heated when required. A great inexpensive idea well worth fitting.

Weather compensation and optimisation enables the controls to detect outside temperatures and adjust the boiler output and water temperature in the heating system accordingly. This promotes better comfort levels and energy efficiency. You can add this sort of system to any existing heating system, although some boilers have it as an integral feature.

Programmable thermostats use a digital clock together with an electronic thermostat and a microprocessor, allowing it to be programmed to give different temperatures at different times of the day. For example, you can set the correct temperature for daytime activity, evening leisure and sleeping. There's often a holiday setting, allowing heating to come on if temperatures drop too low. You can have more than one programmable thermostat added to a system, which coupled with motorised valves give individual control in different parts or zones of the house, for instance upstairs and downstairs.

AIR CONDITIONING:

For a new home you can have air conditioning designed using combined heating and cooling units. It's expensive, complex and, at the moment, not commonly used. More popular are the fresh air systems that rely on extracting warm air from bathrooms and kitchens, recycling it via a heat exchanger and putting it into rooms where heat (and fresh air) is needed. These systems are not strictly speaking air conditioning. They're likely to be used more in future as they're helpful when trying to reduce heat losses via draughts. Warm air heating systems aren't generally popular and can promote dust

VENTILATION:

Mechanical ventilation (an extractor fan) is required in kitchens, bathrooms and WCs and in rooms with no opening window. These get heavy use so make sure they're good quality.

USEFUL TIPS

■ Be specific about what you want

from your design. Make a list of your requirements, for instance - two bathrooms operational at once, lots of hot water, special hot pressure showers.

■ Employ a good, qualified designer and ensure that the people who carry out the work are members of the appropriate bodies so they can issue certificates and commission equipment properly.

■ Make certain that systems are tested and proven to operate at design conditions, and that test certificates, drawings and operating and maintenance instructions are issued prior to payment of final account.

■ Investigate a maintenance contract with the installer.

ELECTRICAL DESIGN

Good lighting makes all the difference to a new home, extension, alteration or refurbishment. These are my suggestions as a result of the many electrical layouts I've dealt with.

Consider a room's lighting requirements in relation to its furniture layout: Draw a plan with furniture to scale so you can superimpose an overlay showing lighting. Such a drawing can also include power points and switch positions. Use symbols to represent lighting and power with an explanatory key. Visualise moving through the room from different directions and having to turn lights on or off. Allow some

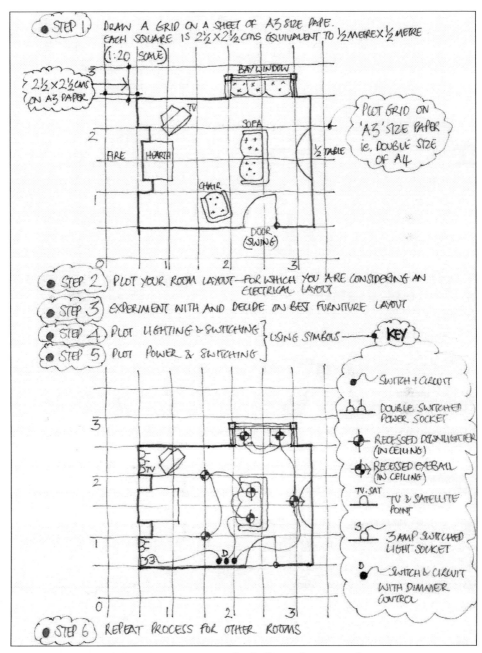

Fig 9.3 How to prepare an electrical layout for your new home

flexibility for changing the room layout. For example, incorporate two or three alternative positions for a TV aerial point or include an adjustable overhead fitting (Fig 9.3). Remember to incorporate facilities for computers and other IT controls – see below.

SELECT A QUALIFIED ELECTRICAL CONTRACTOR

Membership of the NICIEC (National Institution of Electrical Contractors) or the ECA (Electrical Contractors' Association) ensures stringent assessment procedures for their members. In the case of the ECA you also gain the Association's warranty on their members' installations. Membership of these organisations also ensures that electricians provide proper approved test certificates, whether for a minor electrical alteration or a new whole-house installation. At the end of a job (however small) insist on receiving these certificates.

Research the enormous variety of lighting fittings, bulb types and accessories: To achieve creative lighting, establish the desired lighting effect and then select the fittings to attain it. For example:

■ downlighters force light downwards and should be positioned so that they provide light exactly where it's required immediately below

■ uplighters give soft light by reflecting it off a wall or ceiling

■ task lighting is individual fittings which focus on a specific space, such as a desk or workshop bench

■ clear and frosted bulbs produce different effects and bulbs are available in a choice of colours - for instance soft white, sunset yellow or terracotta - which enhance particular décor

■ fluorescent tubes provide good overall illumination cost-effectively

■ halogen and low-voltage lighting have many advantages, including small fittings, overall brightness and producing a sparkle

■ switch plates and plug sockets are available in a range of styles to suit your decoration

■ vpre-set dimming controls enable you to set a particular scene in a room or to recall a particular pre-set light setting at the touch of a button - for example, a kitchen by day, by dusk and by night

THINK ABOUT USING LIGHTING DESIGNERS

There are experts who'll design levels of light and give guidance on the enormous variety of fittings and their effects. Lighting manufacturers can also help with your design.

In addition to lighting and power, your electrical design can incorporate modern home communication networks as part of a home network design.

This enables you to have access to electronic equipment virtually anywhere in the house. It's desirable for any new home to have at least cabling for home communication network and it's likely that building regulations will actually require this in a few years time. Facilities for communication services are normally installed or carcassed at the time building work is being carried out and can include the following:

■ audio

■ telephone

■ security, including door contacts, infrared systems, remote locking

■ TV

■ satellite distribution

■ home automation

■ internet

■ infrared links for remote controls

■ computers

■ close circuit TV (CCTV)

Before preparing your layout, here are some lighting and electrical design ideas I use in each room of a home.

KITCHENS: ELECTRICAL DESIGN

Use downlighters, positioned above work surfaces, and in front of wall cupboards, to direct light onto the kitchen working areas, taking care to avoid shadows. Low voltage or small halogen ceiling eyeball lights work well in kitchens and bathrooms (they make food more colourful and appetising). You can supplement them with under-cupboard lights positioned either at the back of the cupboard or behind a pelmet. Under-cupboard lights give a different effect and can either be used with, or as an alternative to, downlighters. Dimmer controls are easily incorporated in downlighter fittings. Kitchens often now include informal dining areas and are a popular area for families to congregate. To create different atmospheres with lighting, you could focus the lighting on features, such as within a chimney recess or within an enclosure around an AGA or within a glass-fronted cabinet or dresser to provide indirect lighting and a cosy feel. Avoid dark corners by thinking about lighting in relation to the agreed kitchen layout plan. Switching should include dimming control and flexibility in allowing different light systems to be used. Decide whether you want a radio system to allow you to listen in the kitchen or, indeed, any other room in the house.

LIVING ROOM: ELECTRICAL DESIGN

Look for opportunities for lighting to be integrated with a feature fireplace, lower ceiling levels, and structural features such as beams or columns. Inglenook fireplaces look even more impressive with indirect lighting focusing on the fire surround. In your living room you'll almost certainly need lights to read by – position unobtrusive downlighters on a ceiling plane

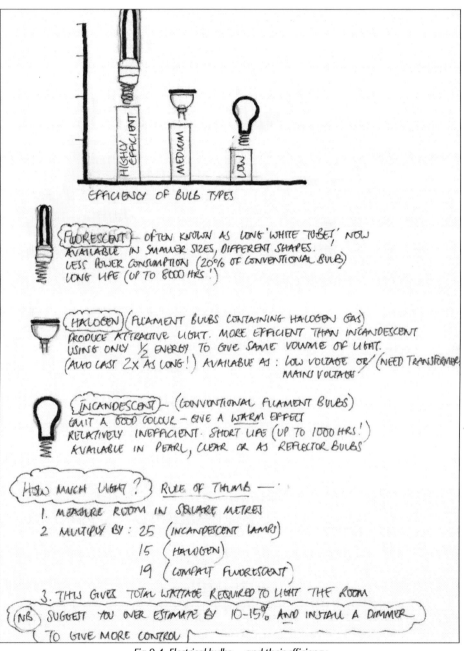

EFFICIENCY OF BULB TYPES

FLUORESCENT — OFTEN KNOWN AS LONG 'WHITE TUBES,' NOW AVAILABLE IN SMALLER SIZES, DIFFERENT SHAPES. LESS POWER CONSUMPTION (20% OF CONVENTIONAL BULB) LONG LIFE (UP TO 8000 HRS!)

HALOGEN (FILAMENT BULBS CONTAINING HALOGEN GAS) PRODUCE ATTRACTIVE LIGHT. MORE EFFICIENT THAN INCANDESCENT USING ONLY ½ ENERGY TO GIVE SAME VOLUME OF LIGHT. (ALSO LAST 2x AS LONG!) AVAILABLE AS: LOW VOLTAGE OR (NEED TRANSFORMER) MAINS VOLTAGE

INCANDESCENT — (CONVENTIONAL FILAMENT BULBS) EMIT A GOOD COLOUR — GIVE A WARM EFFECT RELATIVELY INEFFICIENT. SHORT LIFE (UP TO 1000 HRS!) AVAILABLE IN PEARL, CLEAR OR AS REFLECTOR BULBS

HOW MUCH LIGHT? RULE OF THUMB —

1. MEASURE ROOM IN SQUARE METRES

2. MULTIPLY BY: 25 (INCANDESCENT LAMPS)
   15 (HALOGEN)
   19 (COMPACT FLUORESCENT)

3. THIS GIVES TOTAL WATTAGE REQUIRED TO LIGHT THE ROOM

NB SUGGEST YOU OVER ESTIMATE BY 10-15% AND INSTALL A DIMMER TO GIVE MORE CONTROL

Fig 9.4 Electrical bulbs... and their efficiency

over furniture for reading light as well as general lighting. Alternatively, use task lighting, such as table lights or standard lamps, which can be switched using small 3-pin 5-amp sockets, saving you bending down and fiddling with switches on the lamps themselves. Focus lighting, such as eyeball fittings, allow light to be more directional illuminating a feature or a picture. Maybe conceal lighting behind curtain pelmets. Don't forget to build in flexibility when siting TV's, videos and hi-fi, and remember to run cables inside cabinet carcasses foe speakers (you can have ceiling speakers, if you wish), satellite television for TV and telephone lines for digital TVs.

BEDROOMS: ELECTRICAL DESIGN

Most of the time, bedside lights are enough to illuminate bedrooms. Swing-arm or flexible lamps are excellent for this. Wardrobes should have lighting which operates when a door is opened. Dimmer controls are essential in all bedrooms and think about night lights for children's bedrooms. Provide an evenly distributed light for dressing tables, using brighter light levels for actual dressing areas, tables and reading at bedside.

BATHROOMS: ELECTRICAL DESIGN

I reckon good lighting over a bath and basin is essential, along with a lower general level of light in the room. Make sure that any light above a mirror is central and that any lights mounted either side of it are no more than 750mm (30 inches) apart. Avoid deep shadows on your face looking in a mirror by ensuring light comes evenly from either side rather than overhead. Splash-proof or low voltage splash-proof fittings are preferable. Consider a wired in hairdryer and radio. A good tip is to focus light onto water or glass (mirrors), introducing a sparkle into the room. There should be no switches other than pull-switches in bathrooms for safety reasons. Electric under-floor heating, such as under-tile heaters, adds a luxurious touch.

DINING ROOM: ELECTRICAL DESIGN

Most people choose to have a centre feature light over a dining table. The minimum diameter of a chandelier should be about half the width of the dining table and the bottom of the chandelier should be between 725-850mm (29-34 inches) above the table surface. In rooms with ceilings higher than 2.4 metres (8 feet) you can raise the fixture up to 75mm (3 inches) for each additional 300mm (12 inches) of ceiling height.

HOME OFFICE: ELECTRICAL DESIGN

Position your computer so that the screen doesn't reflect light from windows or ceiling-mounted fixtures. Low-glare luminaires (LG2 Cat 3) would be ideal, or you could use uplighters. Make sure there are adequate power points. Building regulations for new dwellings now require sockets well above skirting level to afford easier access than previously. Think about your needs for all information technology (IT) wiring, including an ISDN line, satellite TV point and fibre optics. If in doubt, put a conduit in with a pull-cord so that any additional facilities can be installed easily at a later stage. BT has many 'home office options', go online and check. Based on your house plans, 'Connect It' will design a cable network into which you can plug computers, modems, telephones, faxes, ISDN, terrestrial, satellite and digital TVs, FM and digital radios, stereo, audio, intercom, baby monitor and CCTV. Total house connection prices depend on house size and individual specification. Think about your needs for information technology (IT) see below.

STAIRS AND HALLS: ELECTRICAL DESIGN

Safety on stairs is paramount. Steps and risers require a good even level of lighting. In addition to ceiling fixtures, consider night-lights at skirting board height. Make a feature of halls with rafter-high ceilings by fitting free-standing or wall-mounted uplighters to draw attention to

the structure and the space. Use energy-saving light fittings for landings where lighting is required over a long period of time.

WORKROOMS: ELECTRICAL DESIGN

Achieve good overall light by using uplighters bouncing light off a ceiling. Bright white halogen lights for detailed close work are very effective. If you have a computer, you need enough light for the keyboard but avoid glare and screen reflection.

GARDEN: ELECTRICAL DESIGN

Paths, porches and steps all need effective illumination. Whilst undertaking building work, take the opportunity to run armoured cable externally to allow lights in flowerbeds to create subtle soft pools of light or floodlights to illuminate larger areas. Lights behind plants can be very effective. A patio area can almost be an additional room to your house, if properly designed and lit. As well as being stylish, exterior lighting is also functional, illuminating paths and steps for safety and security. RCD (residual current device) protection of all external supplies is essential.

SECURITY

Infrared detectors allow lights to be triggered by an approaching person or the onset of dusk. Use halogen floods for intruders as they're very bright and penetrating. It's a good idea to be able to switch external halogen lights in addition to having an infrared detector. This enables you to turn them on from inside the house if you suspect something.

Information Technology (IT):
Connection to the internet. Future for flexibility and ease of connection to the internet is almost certainly going to be via wireless works where you can connect to the internet anywhere where there is a wireless signal. This avoids the use of wires, plug ins and must be the way ahead.

TELEPHONES

This is also going to be via computer links. FM and digital radio, stereo, audio, intercom, baby monitoring, CCTV.

Remote control systems whereby a house can be monitored and manipulated from remote locations.

DRAINAGE SERVICES

Any discussion on services wouldn't be complete without mention foul drainage (the waste that comes from WCs, sinks and wash hand basins) and surface water (rainwater run-off from roofs, garden and drive areas around a home). As with heating, plumbing and electrical services, the same principles for the design of foul and surface water apply to a new home, an extension or even an alteration. Here are the really important design considerations.

CORRECT FALL

Falls (angles at which pipes slope) are governed by the type of pipe and the internal diameter. For most domestic situations a 100mm (4 inch) plastic pipe is the norm and, if plastic is used, the fall shouldn't be less than about 1 in 80. I normally aim for 1 in 40 or 1 in 60.

Don't make the fall too steep or the liquids will run away very fast and leave solids behind, causing blockages.

DIRECTION

As logic suggests, branch runs joining a main drainage run should always join in the direction of flow. Don't let a run flow against the main flow, even though it might gently swing round in the direction of the run.

PROTECTION OF DRAINS

There are rules - both in the building regulations and from the various manufacturers - governing how drains should be laid and how they should be protected. If a drain runs under a building, it's common practice to encase it in concrete and to have movement joints where the drain run moves from being encased in concrete to being just laid in the ground. When a floor is suspended (not resting on the ground), it might be possible to avoid encasing in concrete

ACCESS FOR MAINTENANCE

I've seen so many examples of hidden manholes, not only outside, but inside houses. It's possible to have an internal manhole but avoid this if you can. An internal manhole has to have a specially sealed cover and it's never pleasant to open it in an internal situation. The idea of a manhole is to allow a man easy access. Think about this. If you have a shallow manhole, it can have a smaller opening because access is easier. If it's deeper, it has to be a lot wider - in some cases large enough to allow a man to get inside to do some rodding. Rodding involves clearing blockages using small sections of rod, screwed together to form a long, flexible pole. Blockages do occur because people put things down drains that they shouldn't. If you follow these basic rules, (and you only get one chance to get it right) blockages shouldn't occur and, if they do, they should be easy to clear. Have drains inspected every couple of years. It's worth having the drains cleaned by a specialist firm, usually using high-pressure water jets to clear the scale and deposits that build up over a period of time.

DRAINAGE PROBLEMS

With advances in technology there are now lots of techniques to sort out drainage problems. For example, in the 1960s and 70s builders used materials that have distorted over time. It's possible to ream out these older drains and put a lining inside without actually having to excavate the drain. Various investigations can be carried out using closed circuit television (CCTV) enabling a full inspection and report on an existing drain. When there's a problem with a drainage system on your property, check with your insurance company to see if that eventuality is covered. For example, the use of pitch fibre pipe in the 60s and 70s is usually insurable, if it distorts and causes problems.

DISPOSAL OF FOUL WATER

In urban areas disposal is via sewers and for a new dwelling you'll need permission for connection from the appropriate authority. Connection is a complex job and must be done by an approved contractor carrying public liability insurance for working in a public highway. In rural locations, where there is no mains drainage, the alternative is to use a private system of which there are several types:

■ cesspools are sealed tanks that have to be emptied about every 28 days

■ septic tanks are containers from which water drains off into trench soakaways or a reed bed. Septic tanks won't work in certain soil conditions, so it's necessary to check these before appropriate plant can be selected

■ sewage treatment plants which produce

clean water and need an electrical supply to power their moving parts

Costs vary from £2,000 for a cesspool for a typical house up to £10,000 for a full sewage treatment plant. Over the years I've seen many mistakes and my advice is to connect to a mains sewer, if it's available and, if not, look at the feasibility of a septic tank or sewage treatment plant. A cesspool should always be the last resort. Get specialist advice on the design and installation of a private system.

All private systems require approvals, not only under the building regulations, but also in certain cases from the Environment Agency. Allow adequate time to obtain these consents prior to any work starting. All surface water systems, excluding public surface water sewer connection, require regular maintenance. The building regulations are becoming more onerous in terms of soakaway design and sewage disposal systems. There are serious fines for causing pollution so you must get it right.

SURFACE WATER

The same principles apply to surface water drains. Think about above-ground drainage - guttering should be properly sized to pick up the run off the area of roof space, falls properly set out draining to adequately sized down pipes. From ground level onwards the same principles apply as for

foul drainage but the big difference is the final destination. There are several options. In many rural locations a soakaway (a pit filled with rubble) is the solution. However, in certain soil conditions these just won't work and an alternative has to be found. For obvious reasons, soakaways should be sited away from houses and building boundaries. In urban areas, surface water sewers are usually available to which you can connect your pipework, subject to consent from the appropriate authorities. Rainwater harvesting (see chapter 8) is likely to become a requirement under building regulations.

CENTRAL VACUUM SYSTEMS

While thinking about services, give some thought to including a central vacuum system. You can fit these in an existing home or an extension or incorporate the system as part of a new home construction. To vacuum your home, you insert a lightweight hose into a conveniently located connection point (one point per floor for an average house) and dust is extracted to a central vacuum unit sited away from living areas. It's surprising how easy it is to install these systems and at relatively low cost. They're certainly easier to use than a vacuum cleaner. They're also virtually silent and no dust is allowed to re-circulate, which promotes a cleaner, healthier environment.

CHAPTER 10

DESIGN AND BUILDING COST

The principal design factors that will affect the cost of your project - whether it's a new home, extension or alteration - are the size and shape of the building, the type of construction and the detailing.

SIZE AND SHAPE

The greater the area of a new home or extension the greater the costs. If you want to save money look at reducing area - if you reduce the footprint of a two-storey building this doubles the saving. When I work with clients on the design of their new home or extension, we tend to arrive at an optimum floor area which represents reasonable value for money.

A larger extension will cost more money overall but the unit cost per square foot or metre reduces as the area increases. Conversely, the smaller the area the greater the unit cost.

Building form affects cost. For example, when constructing a house of, say 2,500 sq ft, the cheapest form of construction is a two-storey house, a bungalow is the most expensive, with a chalet bungalow somewhere in between. This is easily explained if you compare a two-storey house with a bungalow of the same floor area. Foundations for each would be a similar depth but the length of the foundations for a bungalow would be

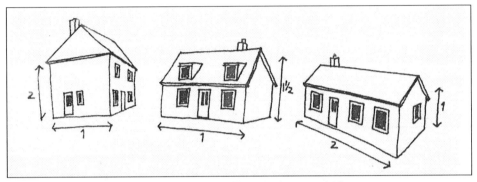

Fig 10.1 Plan shape affects cost (see page 146)

almost twice that of the house. The roof area for a bungalow would be almost twice that of the house. The proportion of circulation space, relative to the area of habitable rooms, would be greater for a bungalow.

Plan shape also influences building cost. A comparison of square and rectangular buildings with the same floor area illustrates the point. The wall-to-floor ratio of the square building is 1.6 whereas the equivalent figure for a rectangular structure is 2.32. The shape of the rectangle requires 45% more wall to enclose the same area; therefore a square building is more efficient in terms of construction cost than is a rectangular one. Plan shape affects cost so remember that irregular shapes, while providing interest and desirable design features, result in increased costs.

TYPE OF CONSTRUCTION

Traditional load-bearing brick and block walls are usually the most cost-effective construction for a new home or extension. This is mainly because in the UK it's the method most familiar to building contractors. In Chapter 7... I described the main types of house and extension construction systems. In general terms, traditional load-bearing brick and block construction costs about the same as timber frame. New technologies are, in many cases, very competitive with traditional construction and timber frame.

The materials you use have cost implications. There are many varieties of bricks, tiles, windows, fixtures, fittings, etc on the market and all have different qualities and prices.

Walls are less expensive than windows so, if you have a lot of large windows, you'll increase cost. The cost of curved wall construction is higher than straight walls. Complex roofs with valleys are more expensive than simple ones. Materials

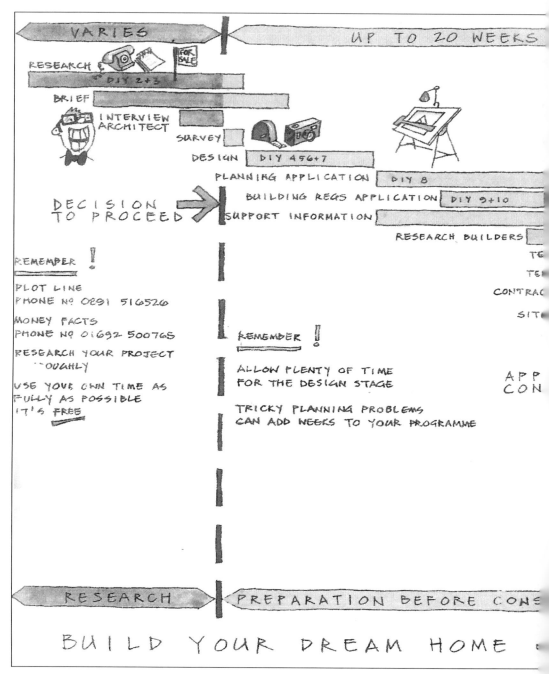

Fig 10.2 Building your dream

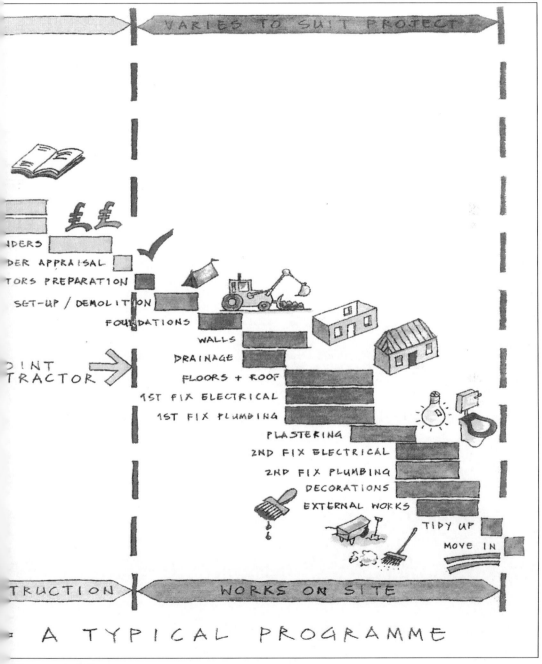

VARIES TO SUIT PROJECT

IDERS
DER APPRAISAL
TORS PREPARATION
SET-UP / DEMOLITION
FOUNDATIONS
WALLS
DRAINAGE
DINT
TRACTOR
FLOORS + ROOF
1ST FIX ELECTRICAL
1ST FIX PLUMBING
PLASTERING
2ND FIX ELECTRICAL
2ND FIX PLUMBING
DECORATIONS
EXTERNAL WORKS
TIDY UP
MOVE IN

TRUCTION   WORKS ON SITE

= A TYPICAL PROGRAMME

home... a typical programme

made by hand are more pricey than mass-produced ones. Construction detail, such as decorative barge boards, corbel brickwork at eaves, stone sills and bay windows all add to overall costs. Open fires are still favoured but fireplaces, chimney breasts and stacks bump up the price. If building costs drives your design, you'll keep everything very simple and avoid any detail. The best approach is to be selective and incorporate detail in locations where it has greatest impact.

OTHER FACTORS

TIME OF YEAR AND LOCAL MARKET CONDITIONS

Contrary to what you might expect, with the UK weather being so unpredictable, building contractors make little or no adjustment for the weather when preparing prices. They might, however, allow extra time on their programme during the winter. You could find a better price quoted for inside work during winter months but the law of supply and demand has the greatest affect upon price. If there's plenty of work around, a builder's profit margin will tend to go upwards. Builders like to plan ahead so they have an advance order book. Most home building projects seem to be urgent and, as soon as planning and building regulations approvals have been

obtained, home owners usually want to get started. Everything must be planned well in advance as it can take about six months from first thoughts to starting on site. Prepare clear and concise information to give the builder confidence that he can undertake the contract smoothly and cost-effectively. Once the extent of work has been agreed, try to avoid making changes. These disrupt the works and give the opportunity for the builder to claim extra costs and extra time to complete it.

SIZE AND TYPE OF BUILDING CONTRACTOR

It's important to select the right builder so ask your home designer to recommend someone. Contractors' building prices include the cost of their general overheads (office, workshop, transport and so on), plus site organisational costs, called 'preliminaries', which include insurance, supervision, unloading of materials, provision of hut, toilet, security, scaffolding, temporary access and reinstatement costs. Generally, builders quote at cost plus 20% - 25% to cover general overheads and organisational costs. These sums are an unavoidable aspect of the total build cost and vary depending on the size of the contractor involved. It's important that you choose an appropriate contractor for the size of the job. For a small project, a small contractor who works on the job personally will provide the supervision without much extra cost. For a larger project (building a reasonable sized detached house, for instance), it's usually safer to employ a larger firm which should be better organised and able to manage a more complex scheme, as well as having backup in event of illness or other unforeseen circumstances.

Rather than approaching several firms, you can negotiate a price with one contractor. When you've decided which builder is the best for the job, it's possible to agree the price on an 'open book' basis. This means you make known your budget and the contractor makes available the build-up of his costs, in order that both can discuss and adjust the work content and specification to reach agreement.

THE HOME DESIGNER

Obtain references for your prospective home designer and make sure he or she isn't on an ego trip, designing totally regardless of budget. It's better to find this out at the start than half way through the job when there's a massive over-spend. Different home designers have different experience and abilities. Check them out before you employ them.

THE SITE

The nature of the site, available space, ground levels, soil conditions, availability of services (water, drains, electricity, gas) all have a significant effect upon the design and construction of any new home or extension. Take advantage of natural features, such as sloping ground and any existing drainage connection, to produce an acceptable but economical solution.

CONTRACT ARRANGEMENTS

Figure 10.2 lists the various types of building contracts I've successfully used - from small home alterations to large extensions and new homes. I can't over-emphasise the importance of producing thorough and detailed information for any building project. This allows you to work out exactly what's required and look at the various options carefully, before anything happens on site. The information can then be set out in the form of written specifications, drawings, schedules, diagrams and so on.

EXTERNAL WORKS

When calculating the cost of your home design, new home or extension, don't forget the costs of external works, such as building paths, patios, planting. Most home owners are aware of the benefits, and added value, of an attractive garden. The cost of creating the setting shouldn't be forgotten in planning any home design project.

VAT

As a general guide, value added tax (VAT) is charged on the total construction cost of any extension or alteration. When you're building a brand new home or creating a new home from an existing building, normally there's usually no VAT to pay. There are complex rules in respect of listed buildings but, in most cases, VAT isn't payable on new works on a listed building, including an extension to a listed building.

CONSEQUENTIAL WORK

Don't forget the knock-on costs associated with alteration works. For example, if you alter one room, it might well affect another, creating the need for redecoration and work like changing radiator positions. Alterations can affect the size of central heating boiler you need and your hot water and electrical systems, giving rise to work that you simply didn't consider at the outset.

AVOID A NEW BUILD... IF YOU CAN

It's usually cheaper to alter an existing building than build a new extension. This all comes back to analysing your requirements properly at the outset to make sure that what you are propose

is the correct design solution. For instance, a room built in the main roof or above a garage can provide additional accommodation for a bedroom, study or teenage annexe. This is why, when I visit people's homes, I always make a point of looking at the whole house so I'm aware of all the spaces available (especially within the roof). When considering your options, do look around to see if there are any other properties that would provide what you want without the need for extending. The answer to this is usually 'no' because of the costs of moving and the price of such property, which are usually far greater than the costs of building an extension or carrying out an alteration. It's, however, worth looking around.

ESTIMATING BUILDING COST

I use three methods for assessing approximate costs for new build, extensions or alterations.

COST PER SQUARE METRE OR SQUARE FOOT

Costs per square metre/foot are supposed to represent a finished shell, which is plastered, decorated, heated and lit. They don't include things like furniture, fittings, carpet, external works, VAT and so on. Cost per square metre/foot vary depending on the area and what you're trying to build. Local building professionals and builders will have a good idea of cost per square foot or per square metre in their area.

COMPARISONS WITH SIMILAR PROJECTS

This is usually quite effective. When considering a new project, look at similar projects recently undertaken in the area for comparison. This gives a good indication of what contractors are charging. Your home designer should have this information from other projects he or she has worked on or use the services of a quantity surveyor (QS).

SIMPLE COST PLAN

A cost plan is really a more thorough way of breaking down the various elements of cost of a building project, applying figures to the various elements of construction. At an early stage figures might only be informed guesses but later on the cost plan will be developed to represent specific areas and rates. Again, get help from your designer or quantity surveyor.

STEP-BY-STEP COST CONTROL

There follows a simple step-by-step guide on how to assess and control building costs through the home design process.

STEP ONE

Make sure you are happy with your home designer.

STEP TWO

Check your requirements before you start building or altering an existing dwelling. This reaffirms the importance of the brief (see Chapter 2) and assessment of the site of a new build or extension properly (see Chapter 3). Don't proceed until you've answered the following questions:

■ have you discussed and confirmed exactly what you require and set out a brief in writing?

■ have you considered alternatives, such as converting a roof space, converting an attached garage or selling up and moving to a larger house?

■ have you considered the implications of VAT on building costs, alterations and extensions? It's often cheaper to knock something down and rebuild it, which saves VAT, than it is to alter and extend it

STEP THREE

Make a quick approximate assessment of the cost of your new build, extension or alteration. Having worked through Chapter 2, you'll have an idea of what you want and the approximate size of rooms. Ask builders locally or speak to your designer about the cost of similar types of project (per square metre or square foot). Apply these rates to accommodation in both ground and upper floors, including external walls. Then, working with your designer if you need help, moderate your price in relation to the following:

■ how much work (if any) you intend doing yourself

■ unusual site conditions, for example, difficult ground conditions, long service runs, expensive access construction

■ complexity of the design - the more dormer windows, glazed screens, decorative brickwork, basements, galleries and so on, the greater the cost

■ professional fees - these depend on the build route you decide to take (see below), however, at this stage, add an overall percentage to cover some involvement from a quantity surveyor, architect or home designer, structural engineer and statutory fees of around 10-15 per cent of the total cost (15-20 per cent for alterations or more complex work)

■ VAT - any alteration or extension attracts VAT at 20 per cent on the total cost (except for listed buildings)

At an early stage, therefore, you'll end up with a very rough guide of overall costs, including VAT and fees. Don't forget the cost of borrowing money and that building costs per square metre or square foot don't include carpets, fixtures and appliances. In the case of building alterations or conversions, it's dangerous to apply cost per square metre or square foot unless you have a directly comparable project, which is rare. What I usually do here is list, in the order that the work will be carried out, a

series of headings, such as:

■ demolition/stripping out

■ new construction works (installation, forming new openings, putting in beams etc.)

■ electrical and mechanical works

■ decorations

The intention is to split the work down into its various elements and assess the costs of each element - they're only provisional figures but it gives you some idea of the likely cost overall. By the end of step three you should have a very rough idea of the likely cost even though, at this stage, the design has not yet been worked out. At this point, assuming you can cope with approximate cost, develop the design as described in preceding chapters and take it on through the planning and building regulation stages (see Chapter 11).

STEP FOUR

Eliminate some of the cost risks and uncertainties. Depending on the nature of the project, this might involve:

■ digging trial holes (see Chapter 3) - ground conditions can have a big effect on cost and to knowledge of what you're building on is an essential part of minimising cost risks in the ground

■ carrying out structural investigations - in the case of alterations, it's often worth hiring a builder for a day to lift floorboards, investigate joist spans and even dig trial holes internally to investigate whether walls have appropriate foundations

■ involving your home designer and possibly having limited input from a quantity surveyor and structural engineer - you don't have to spend a lot of money in buying a few hours of professional time to check your proposals

By now you'll have developed your design, probably obtained planning approval and have made a building regulation application. As a result of this, you'll have a good set of drawings with basic information about the construction. Using that information, your quantity surveyor can produce an initial cost plan. Remember the basic rule - the more detail prepared, the greater the accuracy of cost plan. The quantity surveyor will use experience of the type of building project, local market conditions and various other factors to give you a realistic assessment of cost. However, expect prices to increase rather than decrease as a result of more detailed specifications being developed.

STEP FIVE

Develop a detailed cost plan or, in other words, a detailed description of the various elements you're going to be spending money on. These are usually set out in the order of the building sequence, starting with clearing the site, demolition and working through construction of the project

from new foundations, external walling, floors, roofs, first fix, second fix and so on. A cost is put against each item.

You could prepare your own cost plan, however, unless you've previous experience of building, I strongly advise against this. Getting a quantity surveyor to draw up a cost plan doesn't mean spending an enormous amount of money and the expertise and accuracy that a good quantity surveyor has, it's worth it.

When you're going to be spending anything from £50,000 to half a million, a sound cost plan is the best way to properly manage a project and controlling expenditure. Here are some of the points to consider at the cost plan stage, on which the plan will be based:

■ full site analysis, including trial holes and a structural engineer's comments on foundation type

■ building regulation approval, to eliminate the risk of a building inspector coming back and asking for additional construction features

■ planning permission, which is essential before any project can really get going and there could be planning conditions which might have cost implications, which would have to be assessed in the cost plan

■ construction type will have been considered at the building regulation stage and this should be sufficient for a quantity surveyor to assume a number of construction details, such as decorative brickwork, glazed screens, quality and type of materials

■ home designer's brief, which gives the quantity surveyor a good idea of what you want to achieve so the surveyor can make appropriate allowances

It is, of course, sensible to bear in mind costs throughout the process of developing a design but, at the end of step five, you should be in a position to decide whether you can afford to go ahead or not. But, you might have to adjust the plan.

STEP SIX

Cut and carve to suit the budget. It's relatively easy to look through the cost plan and see where the money's being spent and to make adjustments. I suggest this as a separate step, as inevitably with any project you are going to have to consider changes. These usually mean cutting costs to suit your budget. At this stage, a good home designer might well come up with other ideas, prompted by over-spend, to simplify the design and, in my experience, often improve it.

At any time, even in the early stages, you can approach a builder and ask him to assess costs for you. Remember, though, that builders' costs can be heavily influenced by how much they want the job, how they interpret the design and how convenient the project is to them in terms

of location. It's, therefore, not necessarily an accurate and realistic cost of the project.

STEP SEVEN

Put your plan into action. You now have a design and a realistic cost plan and have made the decision you are able and want to proceed.

First, consider the different build route options. Most people contact three or four builders, give them the information to price up and, usually, accept the lowest tender received (which isn't always the best). However, it's important, before going out to tender (obtaining prices), to prepare a written specification and detailed drawings to accompany the cost plan. This is often termed a 'tender package' and, the more complex the project, the more essential it is to have a really good tender package. For example, such a tender package often includes:

■ either a cost plan, with the figures blank for the builder to fill in, or a written description of work required, in which the builder enters prices against the various items specified

■ a National Building Specification (NBS) specification, which is a description of the elements of works in some detail, referring to the various British Standards of workmanship and materials, and a description of work required, referring back to these British Standards and specification

■ a good set of drawings showing construction detail

The above information takes the project, especially in the case of a new build or an extension, beyond just building regulation or planning approval. There'll be an electrical layout and building details, such as eaves, damp proof course and window frames. This is especially important if one-off new components are being used. Today, with the increased standards of the building regulations and the introduction of what's termed 'robust details' (see Chapter 11), it's absolutely essential that insulation is properly placed at junctions and the element of sealing is properly detailed. It's no good expecting a builder to work to latest standards, you have to show them what's required and ensure it happens on site (that's another story).

OTHER WAYS OF BUILDING YOUR NEW HOME, EXTENSION OR ALTERATION

Other options for building new homes include negotiating a price with the builder or going to a company that will provide what's called a 'turnkey' project, in other words the builder does everything (from design to construction) and hands over the finished house. The turnkey approach isn't necessarily the best or most cost-

effective route. It's certainly convenient to deal with one firm, although the design might not be as well thought through as it would if you employ a good, independent home designer. Going to one company also commits you to its construction type from the beginning

FINDING A BUILDER

Second, find a builder. Before you seek a builder, consider the different routes for building. When going out to tender, have a short list of about six or seven builders in order to end up with four quotes. Your home designer or quantity surveyor normally contacts contractors to assess their interest or you can do this yourself. To find a builder, make enquiries locally, speak to the local authority's building control department, take advice from your home designer or quantity surveyor (if involved) or ask other people who are having work done. Make a short list of builders and then talk to them. Ask for references and follow these up. When you now go out to tender you can proceed with confidence knowing that realistic building costs have already been established. If a price comes in well over budget, it's probably because the builder doesn't want the work.

PARTNERING

An alternative to going out to tender, which I favour, is the partnering approach.

This means involving a builder at an early stage - as early as step one to three above - and then working through the process with that builder. I still recommend using a quantity surveyor because he or she is able to advise you accurately on the reasonableness of the rates the builder quotes. You should be able to establish quite quickly whether the builder is someone you want to work with. Partnering has a number of advantages including:

■ the builder's on board early on enabling him to plan ahead, booking time and resources, rather than going through a last-minute tendering process, when the builder doesn't know whether he's got the job until perhaps a week or two weeks before he's meant to start on site

■ the builder's involved as part of the team in the design process and can contribute his experience and specialist trades to eliminate areas of uncertainty and reduce the cost risk

■ the builder's party to discussions about budget and will realise the project won't proceed if it's over-budget so it's in the builder's interest to make sure it comes in on budget.

CONTINGENCY

Whether working in partnership or going out to tender, you arrive at an actual building cost. To this figure you should add a contingency. A contingency is a sum set aside to cover unforeseen problems that occur in any building project, however well planned. A figure of 5-10% of the building cost is usual. The contingency figure can be kept entirely to yourself or it can be included as part of the overall construction cost. If you choose to keep the contingency fund yourself, realise that in all probability it's going to be spent - don't think of it as money which might be available for other purposes.

PROGRAMME THE WORK

You've now found a builder by whatever process. At this stage, it's appropriate to confirm the job. This can be done by writing a letter of intent, which should be carefully worded. It might also be appropriate to commit some money to cover the builder's initial expenditure. I recommend putting together a building programme at this point. Figure 10.2 shows an example of a typical building programme for a new home and you can see from this the importance of understanding how long the whole project is going to take. Microsoft Project produces a really useful tool for programming works which many builders use. A building programme is an essential tool, not only for you as the customer, but also for the builder. Your interest is to complete the work as quickly as possible

	FEATURE	ADVANTAGES (COST SAVING)
	FIG 10.3 COST EFFECTIVE DETAILS	
1	Open rafter feet	Looks good, saves cost of soffitt, fascia, decorations etc.
2	Rough sawn timber used as cladding, fascias, bargeboards	Low maintenance (as opposed to prepared timber), easy to apply a stain
3	Brackets to columns	Add interest
4	Stop champering to timber joinery columns etc.	Easy to carry out, adds interest and detail
5	Scalloped bargeboards	Easy to do, relatively low cost
6	Use of reconstituted materials classical flagstones instead of real thing, use of double camber lookalike tiles	Readily available, look very convincing
7	Go for quality ironmongery	An item that gets a lot of use and is worth buying quality
8	Designing door linings and door frames to avoid architraves	Saves the cost of supplying and fitting architraves
9	A cheap balcony : achieved by a balustrade being fixed direct to an external wall and doors opening inwards	Saves the cost of constructing a balcony, also allows a view out from a bedside position
10	Flint and stone panels in external walls	Panels allow small quantity of expensive materials which achieve a desirable affect
11	Use of brickwork set out in a quoined fashion at corners	Looks good and introduces a qualty feel to external brickwork

and the builder's interest is the same. If the company does the work quickly and efficiently, it'll make more money. The programme should be realistic and make allowances for inclement weather (excessive snow, wind or rain). If the weather is exceptionally inclement, there could be grounds for the builder to claim an extension to the contract period. The main purpose of the programme is to arrive at a sensible completion date.

BUILDING WARRANTIES OR GUARANTEES

Fourth, invest in a warranty. If you're spending, maybe, tens of thousands of pounds you must have some form of warranty or insurance backed guarantee. This covers you for defects in the structure when the building's finished. There are several insurance or warranty options. Go online and get latest quotes.

Also check what ever professionals you

FIG 10.4 THE BUILDING TEAM	
Home Designers	QUALIFICATION & AREAS OF EXPERTISE
Chartered Architect	(Degree level + post grad.)
	RIBA Royal Institute of British Architects
	ARB Architects Registration Board
	building design, listed buildings, conservation areas
Architectural Technician ˙	MSIAT Member Society of Inst. Architectural Technician
	Technical building help
Interior Designer	ID Degree level MSID
	Design of interiors
Building Surveyor	RICS Degree level
	Technical building design, condition, repair, conversion
	& structure. Listed building conservation areas
Turnkey ˙	Royal Institute of Chartered Surveyors
Cost Advisers	
Surveyor Q/S	RICS degree + post grad.
	Royal Institute of Chartered Surveyors
	Advice on all matters relating to building cost
Building Surveyor	C & Guilds
	HND
Structural Advisor	
C Structural Engineer	ICE Institute of Chartered Engineers
	Matters in relation to building structure
C Building Surveyor	Degree level 3 - 4 yrs.
Drainage Consultant	NBIEW
	All matters in relation to drainage & disposal of sewage
Electrical Designer	Designing electrical layouts
Highway Consultant	C. Eng. New roads, road orders, road enquiries,
	traffic highway safety access

154

Mechanical Services Designer	
Other Professionals:	
& their expertise	
Planning Consultant	RICS or RTPI
	General planning advice, planning law & rules
	Applications, appeals, enforcement, local plan,
	public enquiries, can recommend barristers & other
	specialists.
Highway Engineer	New roads, road orders, road enquiries,
	traffic highway safety access
Landscape Architect	Visual assessment to National Parks, Areas of
	Outstanding Natural Beauty, Countryside & Landscape
	schemes
Solicitor	Public enquiries, challenges decisions in court
	complex legal points
Barrister	Public enquiries, court cases, complex legal points
Building Surveyor	Building designs, condition, repair, conservation,
	structure, listed buildings, conservation areas
Environmental Consultant	Environmental assessment, pollution, nature
	conservation, visual assessment
Ecologist	Wildlife, endangered species, pollution, nature
	conservation, planting & management schemes
Archaeologist	Archaeological remains, schedule ancient monuments,
	areas of archaeological importance, historic towns etc.
Surveyor / Estate	Supply & demand for accommodation & land market
	trends, occupation of property

use have indemnity insurance to cover them against any mistakes they might make in their advice or design work.

BUILDING CONTRACTS

Sign a building contract. My advice is to always have a contract, how ever small the project. Various forms of contract are available covering the essentials, such as cost, start and completion dates, insurance, payment and damages. Standard forms of building contracts are produced by Joint Contracts Tribunal (JCT) and are available from most building bookshops and online.

The JCT Home Owner's Contract for alterations is a very simple pamphlet document covering the basics including payment, warranties and damages for not completing on time. Damages are money payable deductible by the client if the job doesn't finish in accordance with what's been agreed. In my experience, it's very difficult to actually get damages in the event of disagreement. However, I always suggest that there's some form of long stop, by way of a damages clause, so there's an incentive to finish. Talking of which, another way to tackle this issue is to consider an incentive payment for finishing on time. This is a better way of dealing with a project, especially if you're partnering. The JCT Home Owner's Contract covers most of the basics and is an easy to understand document.

The JCT Minor Works Contract is appropriate for projects up to around £100,000, although this depends on the complexity of the contractual arrangements. The Minor Works form relies on the involvement of a Contract Administrator, whether this is an architect, surveyor or some other professional. It's a good workable contract which, again, makes provision for the building contract essentials.

If the cost of works is greater than £100,000, you can use the JCT Intermediate Form of Contract, which is more comprehensive and appropriate to a medium-size domestic building contract. It's essential to have a proper contract with a project of this size and to have it administered by someone experienced in using it.

CHAPTER 11

REGULATIONS AND DESIGN

PLANNING PERMISSION

New houses, conversions and some alterations to existing houses require planning permission from your local council. Two of the main factors the councils take into account are the appearance of the building and the layout of the site. Therefore, the requirement for you to get planning permission can have a significant influence on your design. Most new building work needs planning permission but, within certain specified limits, some extensions and residential outbuildings are exempt from the need to apply. The types of work and limits are specified in a government document (General Permitted Development Order) which sets out householders' 'permitted development rights'. It's is a complex document so ask your home designer or consultant for guidance.

Councils judge designs submitted for planning approval against their planning policies and guidelines. Government also publishes planning guidance, which should also be taken into account. Council policies on design are contained in documents called local plans or unitary development plans (UDPs), which you can inspect at your local district or city council offices (in England these are being replaced over the next few years by new-style local development frameworks, and by local development plans in Scotland and Wales). The council's planning officers can refer you to the relevant policies and your home designer or consultant should be familiar with them. Government policies apply throughout the respective country (ie England, Northern Ireland, Scotland and Wales). These are general in nature and copies of the documents should be available from your local council on request or on the various branches of governments' websites.

Planning policies are intended to protect the interests of neighbours, future occupiers and prevent harm to the appearance of the area. Consequently, they're concerned with such issues as ensuring privacy between homes, achieving satisfactory relationships between buildings, in terms of height, location, style and providing safe vehicular access. These are largely design issues and mostly affect external appearance rather than internal arrangements.

One fundamental distinction planning policies do make is over the places where new homes can and can't be built. In most local plans, boundary lines are drawn around towns and villages. Inside these boundaries houses can normally

be built and outside they normally can't. This is to protect the countryside from being built on and to ensure houses are built where facilities are available. I recommend, no matter how simple a scenario might appear, that you check with the council, rather than presume planning permission is or isn't required. There are some quite complex criteria to check so write to the local authority explaining what you want to do and ask the officers to confirm in writing whether or not permission's required.

PLANNING APPLICATIONS

Planning application procedure is beyond the scope of this book but is covered fully in How to Get Planning Permission in the same series. I'll focus on the design aspects of your proposal and how to put these across in your planning application.

The time it takes to work up a design and prepare an application can be weeks or months of hard (but enjoyable) work. The formal planning application process is probably going to take about eight weeks to get a decision from the council. It, therefore, pays to get it right first time. Design is a principal element of an application so it's essential to work with a good home designer, who's sympathetic both to your needs and to the council's requirements.

Good presentation of an application

is vital and a good home designer will advise you on the type of presentation and content needed for your particular scenario. For some years I've served on the architecture panel of a council, advising planning officers on design issues of significant and controversial planning applications. This has confirmed to me that presentation is a key aspect in the success of applications, especially simple things like the information being clear and easy to understand and showing the proposal in context with surrounding buildings and landscape features. A simple model or a perspective drawing always provides a quick and easy way to communicate what's being proposed.

These are some suggestions for making planning applications for a new home, extension or alterations more likely to succeed:

■ colour at least one copy the drawings, for the building and also the surrounding environment so the scheme can be seen in context
■ get a three-dimensional models made, which can be simple card models and needn't be expensive
■ include a simple perspective drawing as small, simple, sketch views give convey a lot of information
■ incorporate artistic flair in the drawings, such as shading and

landscaping, to make the scheme look attractive – basic outline drawings and some computer aided design (CAD) can look stark

There are a number of specialists who can come in and help with a particular aspect of an application in respect of a home. If there's a strong garden design element then a landscape architect or garden designer should prepare a scheme as part of the application. Where there's an access issue, consider commissioning a report from a highway engineer. If there are significant planning issues, involve a planning consultant to write a statement about the planning issues and your proposals. When a building has historic interest, speak to a local historical society with a view to getting support the proposals. In the case of a listed building, you might be required to have an archaeological survey carried out to ensure the important historical features of the building wouldn't be adversely affected.

All supporting information you submit as part of a planning application - I title this package a 'Planning Statement' – should be bound together so that it doesn't get lost. I always include a good set of photographs of the site so that the planning officer, and anyone the officer consults, can get a good feel for the place. Not all consultees get time to actually visit the site. Try to imagine you are a planning officer. What you're trying to do is to make his or her job easier by providing clear, well presented information that's easy to understand. The application should answer all the queries that any planning officer is going to have. Does it comply with policy? Does it achieve a satisfactory relationship in terms of height, location, style and providing safe vehicular access? And so on.

DESIGN STATEMENTS

Design Statements are increasingly a requirement of local authorities for planning applications. A Design Statement is a written document setting out the design principles adopted for the proposed development, together with illustrative material, where appropriate, demonstrating how the design solution proposed would respect and benefit the local environment. Design Statements are helpful with any planning applications, however small - the statement can be very brief for a modest scheme. The requirement for a Design Statement was originally derived from government planning guidance but is now included in many council's planning policies. Design Statements are needed to help planning officers, members of the public and councillors to understand the factors that influence the design, to explain how the design benefits the local environment and to assess the design against local plan policies, supplementary planning guidance and government guidance.

I find Design Statements help minimise the potential for costly and time-consuming re-design once the application is submitted. Many councils realise the capacity of a site for development can only be properly tested through the design process and producing a Design Statement is a fundamental part of this process. Producing a Design Statement for a typical house usually involves:

■ looking at the site and surroundings and identifying the physical factors which make your site and local area distinctive. For instance, this could include the design of existing buildings, the amount of space between you and your neighbours, any trees, boundaries, and the size, roof form, architectural style and materials of the existing house (if any)

■ identifying the other factors that will influence the design of your extension or alteration or new home such as local plan policies and any supplementary planning guidance

■ explaining how your proposed design

relates to the design principles you have identified and how it will benefit the local environment.

So, for a typical new house or extension to an existing house, the Design Statement should include:

■ a brief written statement clearly identifying the factors which have led to the proposed design solution

■ plans and elevations of the proposed design, including details of adjoining buildings, spacing between buildings and a street scene elevation where appropriate

■ photographs, where appropriate, to illustrate the site and its surroundings

Finally, I have summarised steps I take before, during and after making a planning application, whether this is a new home, extension or alteration.

APPLICATION MAKING PROCESS

Pre-planning enquiry I always try to arrange a meeting with a local planning officer to discuss the proposals, however small or simple. As a home designer, I'm not necessarily aware of all policies and standards in a particular area. I'm might not know of planning precedent that might have been set recently that might influence a planning department to resist or support an application. At an early stage, involve the planning officer, who's likely to deal with the application right through from start to finish. It's at this time I might show the planning officer some very preliminary sketches. The scheme could be larger than you, the home owner, might actually want. Psychologically, it can be helpful to be seen to reduce the scale and size of the scheme during the negotiating process.

REVIEW APPLICATION CONTENT

This depends on the particular scheme being presented. Review carefully basic requirements for the planning application, such as plans, elevations, sections, location plan, block plan, and then think hard about what information is relevant in this particular proposal. Go over the various points mentioned above and decide what sort of additional information might be required. Consider whether there's a need for expertise, maybe a highway engineer or planning consultant.

SUBMIT AND MONITOR

The planning officer might not actually look at the application for several weeks so make a diary note to phone him or her after two or three weeks from the date of submission. Where necessary, I go to see the officer involved and discuss any concerns. Planning officers might not have reached any firm conclusions at this stage – they'll always cover themselves anyway by saying they still need to get feedback from consultees. The council is obliged, with most home design schemes, to consult the parish/town/community council, any conservation area groups and other interest groups. Ask the officer what such groups have said or go in to the offices to look at the application file. It's often possible to provide additional information or to alter the scheme to try to prevent concerns turning into reasons for refusing an application.

WITHDRAWAL

As an applicant, up to the very last minute before a planning decision is issued you can withdraw an application to avoid getting a refusal. However, there's usually little point in doing that because a withdrawn application remains on the council's records and withdrawal prevents the possibility of making an appeal.

PLANNING MEETING

Most local authorities allow the applicant and/or agent (planning consultant or home designer) to speak in support of an application at planning committee meetings, within a defined time slot (typically 2-3 minutes). Objectors can

also speak. If you're prepared to do this, it can help, not least by countering any objections made. Planning committee meetings are open to the public so you can always just attend and listen to the discussion.

DECISION

With luck one receives planning approval and this accompanied by planning conditions. These include a time limit of three years to start the work and getting council approval of samples of materials is fairly standard. There might be conditions requiring more information related to design issues, such as landscaping or type of windows, especially when the building has historic interest. Remember, it's your responsibility to make sure conditions are complied with or discharged (the latter usually has to be confirmed in writing by the council).

BUILDING REGULATIONS

Building regulations ensure your home is constructed properly and doesn't threaten your health and safety. They have a fundamental effect on home design, both new homes and extensions or alterations to existing ones. The main areas covered by the regulations are fire safety, ventilation, hygiene, drainage and conservation of fuel and power.

FIGURE 11.1 TIPS FOR DEALING WITH PLANNING PROBLEMS

1   If you are being criticised for bulk, size, impact, a way a proposal will just not fit in then what about an underground home? In certain locations and especially sloping sites underground homes can provide a planning solution which is very difficult to argue against!

2   When you are up against the allegation of 'overdevelopment' it can be worth going in with less and getting any form of planning permission. If you have time you can then go back and ask for more. This is what I term the ratchet approach and it has proved very successful over the years where there is time to 'work on a development' over a period of years. I can think of many examples where I've obtained a planning permission in say over a 5 or 10 year period that I would have never been considered if it were submitted as an initial application.

3   Remember the concept of a three-storey bungalow. Many applications are constrained due to a two-storey building being visually unacceptable or not fitting in with the local environment. This is where a bungalow with a sufficient ground floor footprint can often include a basement and a roof conversion giving in effect three storey accommodation.

4   A fresh approach. Planners and Local Councils can often get frustrated or bored with a particular design approach or presentation. It can make all the difference to change your home designer and provide a completely different approach, different presentation, different angle on the same design problem. I spent 4 years on a Architect's Advisory Panel to the Local Authority giving design advice to Planning Officers. Believe me, a fresh approach to design can make all the difference to the way in which an application is received.

5   Historic buildings, conservation areas. A discussion on planning would not be complete without mention of historic buildings, conservation areas. These are looked at particularly closely and Councils have a greater control over design in these cases. If work is proposed that would affect the historic or architectural interest of a listed building (internally or externally) a separate application called 'listed building consent' is required. Listed building consent is sometimes required when planning permission is not as, for example repairs and alterations could affect the interest of the building. Councils designate conservation areas over historic and / or unique parts of towns or villages. The Council can tell you whether your building is listed or is in a conservation area. there are more restricted permitted development rights for listed buildings and in conservation areas. Where a historic building or area is involved the Council expect the original character of the building or area to be respected. This means original features cannot be removed or obscured, building materials have to be as close to the original as possible and additions must
 usually be smaller and not change the basic proportions of the main dwelling. Councils have Conservation Officers or Advisors (usually Architects) and it is worth discussing your design ideas with them at an early stage.

Building regulations are contained in a detailed set of documents (called 'approved documents') which are generally well written and illustrated, and available from HMSO (see homedesignonline.co.uk directory). I don't suggest investing (what's a fair amount of money) in these documents, as they need updating constantly, and you can view them online instead.

Local authority building inspectors enforce the regulations (in London the arrangements are slightly different) but there are alternatives - you can use other 'approved inspectors' or organisations, such as the National House Builders' Confederation (NHBC). In most cases I find the local authority to be best set up and organised to deal with extensions, alterations and new homes. The NHBC tends to deal more with the developer market.

WHEN BUILDING REGULATIONS APPLY

Detached buildings

Detached buildings are exempt from the building regulations if they have:
■ floor area up to 15 square metres and contain no sleeping accommodation
■ floor area up to 30 square metres, contain no sleeping accommodation and are wholly 1 metre or more from all boundaries

■ floor area up to 30 square metres, contain no sleeping accommodation and are constructed substantially of non-combustible materials
■ greenhouses

Extensions

The following extensions are exempt from the building regulations:
■ conservatories with a floor area not exceeding 30 square metres when they're at ground level and fitted with safety glazing
■ porches with a floor area not exceeding 30 square metres at ground level and fitted with safety glazing where appropriate
■ car ports with a floor area not exceeding 30 square metres at ground level and open on at least two sides

Alterations

Some minor works are exempt and some aren't:
■ repair work is exempt where elements are replaced with the same, or similar, materials by way of repair, for example, a flank wall or a bay or the whole of a roof where a defective timber beam is replaced by a steel beam
■ underpinning is covered, unless the building or extension being underpinned is exempt
■ replacing roof tiles or slates is

covered, unless it's with the same or similar materials

■ loft conversions are covered where a room is formed in the roof space, whether it's a habitable room or not and whether it has a stairway or not

■ replacement windows are covered and some replacement doors

■ new fittings – some are covered including basins, WCs, baths, showers and sinks, unless they replace existing fittings in the same room

■ making a new bathroom or kitchen of an existing room is covered

■ installation of solid fuel, oil or gas-burning heating appliances is covered

■ structural alterations, such as forming an opening in an existing load-bearing wall (some timber frame walls are load-bearing) or an existing opening is widened, is covered

HOW BUILDING CONTROL WORKS

Building work is inspected by local authority building inspectors as it's carried out, to make sure it complies with the building regulations. Inspections need to be carried out on several occasions - at the start and completion and before some of the works are covered up. For instance, inspectors look at excavations for foundations, foundation concrete, damp proof

courses and over-site concrete, drains, the structure of floors and roofs, principal beams, steel and reinforced concrete. A test of new drainage is also carried out to show that it doesn't leak. The home owner or person carrying out the work has to tell the local authority when these stages are reached. If the building inspector is happy with the work, the council issues a completion certificate. Where the inspector isn't satisfied, he'll tell you why and advise on resolving the problem. When you sell your house you'll almost certainly be asked to produce a completion certificate for work done and, if you don't have one, you could have difficulty selling. There's a regularisation procedure to deal with this situation.

HOW THE REGULATIONS AFFECT YOUR DESIGN

NEW HOMES AND EXTENSIONS

Any construction system must be structurally stable, keep water out and retain heat to a given standard. The regulations are now going to include air-tightness, to prevent heat losses through gaps in construction. This is why, when demolishing and rebuilding a home, you achieve much higher standards of construction than by trying to adapt and upgrade an existing building.

WINDOW AND DOOR OPENINGS

The regulations control the amount of window area and ventilation for particular habitable rooms. The standard of double-glazing is controlled and there are requirements to provide air vents as part of the structure. This includes replacement glazing, which is the complete replacement of one or more windows, rooflights, roof windows or doors that are at least half glazed. You're obliged to involve either The Fenestration Self-Assessment Scheme (FENSA) or the building control department. One of the building regulations approved documents (L) gives guidance on the insulation values for glazing, which require a higher standard of insulation than can be achieved with simple double glazing. There's also a requirement for toughened or laminated glass where the glazing is near the floor or ground.

FLOORS

Floor construction is controlled in terms of resisting moisture coming up from below, thermal insulation and, in certain cases, sound insulation.

DRAINAGE

Regulations cover both foul and surface water drainage, above and below ground. They control the type of material used, access for maintenance (eg number and size of manholes) and fall.

HEATING SYSTEMS

These are controlled under recent regulations in terms of boiler type and efficiency and also apply to changing your boiler. Regulations cover the type of boiler, the type of fuel (whether this be oil, gas or solid fuel), the arrangements for fuel supply and the combustion and flue arrangements. These requirements can be met by employing suitably qualified plumbers who are registered with the various authorities governing the particular fuel which the boiler uses. For example, if you have a gas appliance the person working on it should be Corgi registered; if it is oil, they should be registered by Oftec. Where this is the case, the regulations stand back and accept that your system will comply with the regulations.

FIRE MEANS OF ESCAPE

The regulations affect distances travelled before a person can get to a safe area or out to open air. They affect window size at first floor level, if they're what's termed an escape window, and they affect the layout of a home, for example, where a staircase discharges into a habitable room, there might be a problem in terms of means of escape from the first floor.

ACCESS

The regulations have changed in recent years to ensure home designs make life easier for disabled or partially disabled individuals. Points like making sure internal doors are wide enough for wheelchairs, WCs can be accessed by someone in a wheelchair and entrance approaches and door thresholds are suitable for disabled access. Power points and switches have to be located within a wall zone that avoids someone having to bend right down.

Access to the house

An approach from a car parking, either on or off the plot, to the front door should be level or ramped where this is reasonable. Sometimes these requirements can be switched to be another door instead. There's no control over land outside the plot. The surface finish, gradient, width and provision of landings and ramps are controlled. Hand rails aren't required with this type of access but an accessible threshold is required to the door. In other cases, a suitable stepped approach can be used with a hand rail one side and an accessible threshold is not then essential. In either case, a minimum

entrance door width is specified. Accessible thresholds (where the entrance is almost level) need careful design to ensure rain can't get into the house and this applies to both traditional doors and frames or purpose-built items.

Access within the house

The regulations cover widths of doorways and corridors on the ground floor. Accordingly, obstructions such as radiators need to be located carefully. Heights of switches and sockets are controlled as are stairways in split level houses but there are concessions for town houses.

WC

Your design should incorporate a ground floor WC with basin suitable for use by a person in a wheelchair. The layout of the toilet, basin, and any obstruction, such as heated towel rails, needs careful planning, particularly if the cubicle is small. There's no requirement for support rails in a house and the cubicle can be considerably smaller than those provided in public buildings. It needn't be large enough to fully accommodate a wheelchair.

Access pitfalls

■ basins larger than their representation on drawings

■ lost width due to dimensions being structural rather than allowing for the thickness of plaster

■ nowhere to put radiators which were omitted from drawings

■ inadequate clear doorway openings because the thickness of the doors themselves was not taken into account

■ making WCs and corridors as small as possible leaving no margin for error

■ poor threshold arrangements due to inadequate designs or drawing details not being adhered to

DEMOLITION OF BUILDING

You may need to give notice to the local authority before demolishing a building or part of a building. To what demolition work does this apply? Demolition of the whole or part of a building except there are exceptions and if in doubt you need to ask your local authority.

LOFT CONVERSIONS

Building regulations apply to loft conversions. There is more to it than might, at first, be apparent. The main issues are:

Means of escape in case of fire

Most loft conversions involve increasing the number of storeys of the dwelling from two to three. Invariably the escape route from the new storey will be via the stairway. If there is a fire in a room on the ground or first floor and the stairway becomes-smoke logged this escape route will be unusable and there will be no way out unless an alternative exists.

Alternative escape routes are mostly impractical for dwellings; alternative external escape routes are normally through a window roof light or external balcony. Building regulations will require protection to the stairway using equipment such as self-closing doors, fire doors and smoke detectors. The escape route will normally need to be separated from all other rooms in the house, all the way to an external door. An arrangement where a lounge is open plan to the stairway is normally not acceptable. Smoke detectors need to be mains powered for maximum reliability and effectiveness. They will normally be sited in the stairway, one per storey. In certain circumstances an alternative escape route can be considered via a suitably located window roof light or balcony.

Fire resistance of floors

The following is relevant to lofts: the ceiling under the loft will need to give adequate fire resistance to protect the new floor. Usually the ceiling will be adequate but occasionally it will need to be upgraded, particularly if it is not of plasterboard or sound lathe and plaster.

The strength of a new floor

The existing ceiling joists were invariably not intended to support more than occasional storage loads and will not be strong enough to support a floor and the imposed loads that can be expected so a new floor will most likely be needed. The floor itself needs to be supported, often on steel beams spanning onto existing load bearing walls. Struts from the purlins under the rafters (or roof structure) will probably need to be removed so that the roof can be supported in an alternative way. New floor joists will then need to support these additional loads. The existing internal walls and lintels in internal and external walls will need to be checked and possibly replaced before applying additional load. As additional loading is put onto the external walls the foundations need to be adequate to support that additional load. It is worth checking these things out at an early stage as there may be a need to underpin existing foundations, which could significantly affect your decision to proceed.

Access to loft rooms

Retractable loft ladders are not suitable.

A stairway will normally be provided to serve the new storey but in exceptional circumstances (where space does not permit a conventional stairway) an alternating tread stair or fixed ladder may be acceptable.

Roof void ventilation

A void in a roof above thermal insulation needs to be ventilated. When a loft is converted roof void insulation needs to be considered. Ventilation openings may need to be added to the eaves and the ridge and space for air-flow above insulation to sloping ceilings needs to be provided. It is normally better to provide full working drawings than make an application for a loft conversion via a building notice.

PARTY WALL ACT 1996

This is nothing to do with building regulations, but the Act provides a framework for preventing and resolving disputes in relation to party walls, boundary walls and excavations near neighbouring buildings. It covers:

■ Work on an existing wall shared with another property or
■ Building on the boundary with a neighbouring property or
■ Excavating near a neighouring building
You should find out whether the work falls within the scope of the Act.

If it does, you must serve a statutory notice on all those defined by the Act as adjoining owners. A notice must be given even when the work will not extend beyond the centre line of the party wall. The professional bodies usually willing to help are: The Royal Institute of Chartered Surveyors; Architecture & Surveying Institute; The Association of Building Engineers; The Royal Institute of British Architects.

FIRE

Fire detection and alarm systems. Smoke alarms can significantly increase the level of safety by automatically giving an early warning of fire. Smoke alarms are normally fitted in circulation spaces, halls and landings, between bedrooms and places where fires are mostly likely to start (kitchen and livings rooms) at least one on every floor. They should be sited in accordance with manufacturer's instructions and be positioned so as to be accessible for maintenance. The building regulations will normally require smoke alarms to be fitted to new buildings and to existing buildings which are extended, have their lofts converted to living accommodation or undergo material change of use.

ESCAPE WINDOWS

Many lives are saved by escape through windows in the event of fire, either unaided or with the assistance of the fire brigade, or a neighbour, using a ladder. On the ground or first floor a window can be used for escape if it is suitably located and has a suitably sized opening. From above the first floor escape through windows is less practical due to the height of the drop to ground level so the internal stairway will normally be protected against fire in rooms (with fire doors).

As far as the building regulations are concerned, if you replace a window the regulations will apply. If a window is presently suitable for escape the replacement should be no less suitable unless the building has adequate means of escape disregarding the presence of the window. Particular consideration needs to be given to the clear opening size. Many modern windows open in such a way that the clear unobstructed opening is considerably smaller than the opening in the surrounding framework. Guidance is that to be suitable for escape a window should have an unobstructed area that is at least 0.33 square metres and at least 450cm high and 450cm wide.

WINDOW LOCKS

Most modern windows can be locked shut. Security against breaking in and keeping children from climbing out needs to be balanced carefully against means of escape in the case of fire. Consider carefully where to keep keys. At least keep a key in every room that has a locked window (through which escape is possible). Keep it where it cannot be seen or reached from outside and, if appropriate, where children cannot reach it.

RECENT CHANGES TO THE BUILDING REGULATIONS

The Building Regulations are updated periodically, with some updated more frequently than others. A qualified professional (Architect or Surveyor) will keep themselves up to date with these changes and be well-placed to help guide you through the process.

The most recent changes to the Building Regulations took place in 2010. These included Part G (Hygiene), Part F (Ventilation), Part J (Combustion Appliances and Fuel Storage Systems), and Part L (Conservation of Fuel and Power). The changes to Part G cover the supply of cold water, measures to further increase water efficiency in new build houses (following the introduction of a tighter Government climate change strategy), and the supply and storage of hot water, which includes measures to prevent scalding.

The greatest changes occurred within Part L to help meet the zero carbon target for all new homes by 2016. This will mean that buildings will need more insulation, more low energy lighting, and - perhaps most importantly- will need to include renewable energy sources (solar panels, heat pumps, etc.) to demonstrate compliance. These requirements mean buildings will become increasingly airtight with the greater levels of insulation required, and as such Part F has been amended to ensure that sufficient ventilation is provided for the occupants of buildings. Part J has been amended to take account of the need for ventilation to supply appliances with open flues (wood burning stoves, coal fires, etc.), and the need for Carbon Monoxide detection for all new and replacement solid fuel appliance installations.

MAKING A BUILDING REGULATION APPLICATION

I have therefore listed below my step-by-step guide in making a building regulation application. I suggest you start this after planning approval has been granted. The reason for this is that if you forge ahead and make a building regulation application without having first obtained planning permission all the work could be wasted, if the plans are turned down or changed.

STEP ONE

Get professional help. It may well be that the person who has made your planning application can go on and make the appropriate applications under the building regulations. The documents are complex, numerous and are being changed. To expect you, the home owner, to buy all these documents, understand them and make your own application is quite a task!

STEP TWO

For a new home or any significant alterations or extensions, the local authority building control department will require you to obtain and submit proper calculations by a fully qualified structural engineer. Most home designers, architects and surveyors will not actually have this expertise and you will need to go to a structural engineer for help. Your home designer will, undoubtedly, be able to recommend someone but you must employ that person directly, so that if there are any problems you have a direct contract with that person.

STEP THREE

Your home designer will make the application on your behalf as your agent (you remain the applicant as with planning). The application usually consists of a package of drawings and notes showing basic specifications to comply with the regulations. Please note this not a full written specification. The building regulations do not cover electrical works, decorations, fitting of kitchens, bathrooms and so on. So don't expect a set of building regulation application drawings to be an indication of total construction cost. It won't be! The application, when received the local authority, is then checked by the building inspector who is usually the same person that will visit the site at a later stage during construction. It usually takes about three or four weeks for the inspector to look at the application and then come back with any queries. (This will vary according to which authority checks the application). With most applications there will be a list of queries that will need answering either by the home designer or by the structural engineer. Generally, after this stage the application is approved, somewhere around six weeks from the date of the original submission. You are entitled to start the work once you have submitted the application but I always advise people to wait until full approval has been given before starting. When approved the building inspector will send your home designer an approval notice, together with cards that need to be filled in at the various stages of construction. Your home designer should give you a copy of this approval for your file as it is an important document and will be required at some future date when you sell the house.

Remember, the building inspector, despite checking the drawings and visiting the site, doesn't actually take any responsibility for checking work so it is usually still necessary to have your own surveyor, architect, home designer on the job.

STEP FOUR

Once you have building regulation approval the works then commence on site and it is the builder's responsibility to give the local authority building inspector (if this is the route you have chosen) suitable notice (usually a couple of days) before starting work.

The building inspector will then visit the site at key construction stages such as excavation of foundation before casting of concrete, dpc (damp proof course) height above ground floor, floor slab design and roof structure. They will also usually carry out a drainage test. It is important that your home designer works with, and cooperates with, the building inspector. If there is a clash of personalities, which there often is, this is not in your best interest. Encourage co-operation wherever possible.

STEP FIVE

The final inspection. As a home owner you must make sure (your home designer should remind you of this) that a final inspection is carried out by the building control officer and that this inspection is confirmed to be satisfactory in writing. Solicitors now look for this when a property is sold and it is particularly important in the case of a new home or an extension to see that the work has been approved, checked and signed off by the building control department. If it hasn't there could be serious delays when it comes to sale.

Also Available

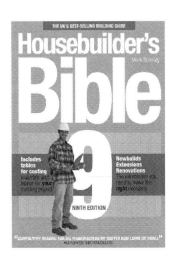

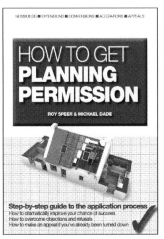

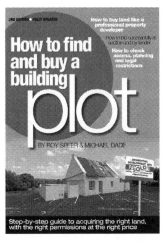

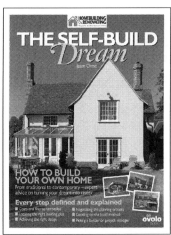

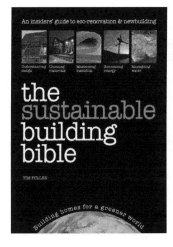

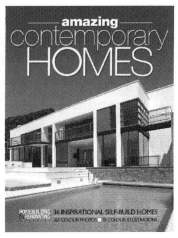

www.ovolobooks.co.uk

Printed in Great Britain
by Amazon